PROFESSIONAL
LIABILITY/RISK
MANAGEMENT
A MANUAL / FOR SURGEONS

Edited by Paul F. Nora MD, FACS

DEVELOPED BY
THE PROFESSIONAL LIABILITY COMMITTEE
AMERICAN COLLEGE OF SURGEONS

The opinions expressed in this manual represent the views of professional experts and, as such, do not constitute policy of the American College of Surgeons. The Table of Contents and subject material were determined by the members of the College's Professional Liability Committee.

© 1991 American College of Surgeons
55 East Erie Street
Chicago, IL 60611-2797
All rights reserved
Library of Congress Card Catalog Number: 91-33135
ISBN 0-9620370-8-7

TABLE OF CONTENTS

PROFESSIONAL LIABILITY COMMITTEE v
LIST OF CONTRIBUTORS vii
ACKNOWLEDGMENTS xi
   I. **BACKGROUND AND INTRODUCTION TO THE MANUAL** 1
  II. **SUBSTANTIVE TORT LAW** 7
       Historical Review.. 11
       Current Medical-Legal Concepts 17
       Efforts to Reform and Change 67
 III. **RISK FINANCING** 93
 IV. **RISK PREVENTION** 105
       Surgeon-Patient Relationship 109
       Consent and the Process of
          Informed Consent 115
       Proper Documentation—
          The Medical Record 125
       Office and Outpatient Settings.................. 129
       Departments of Surgery........................... 135
       The Resident.. 143
  V. **CLAIMS MANAGEMENT** 153
       Surgeon-Attorney Relationship 157
       The Deposition... 165
       The Trial... 173
       Settlement 185
       Protecting One's Assets 191
 VI. **THE PSYCHOLOGICAL TRAUMA OF A MEDICAL
      MALPRACTICE SUIT: A PRACTICAL GUIDE** 197
GLOSSARY 213
INDEX 241

PROFESSIONAL LIABILITY COMMITTEE

This manual has been developed through the efforts of the Professional Liability Committee of the American College of Surgeons.

Chairman
   Frank C. Spencer, MD, FACS, New York City

Committee Members
   Alfred J. Clementi, MD, FACS,
     Arlington Heights, IL
   John E. Connolly, MD, FACS, Irvine, CA
   Joseph B. Davis, MD, FACS, Marion, IN
   M. Martin Halley, MD, JD, FACS, Topeka, KS
   William W. Kridelbaugh, MD, FACS, Albuquerque
   George D. Malkasian, Jr., MD, FACOG, FACS,
     Rochester, MN
   Barry M. Manuel, MD, FACS, Boston
   Ian Nisonson, MD, FACS, Miami
   Andrew H. Patterson, MD, FACS, New York City
   Richard L. Rovit, MD, MSc, FACS, New York City
   David C. Sabiston, Jr., MD, FACS, Durham, NC

ACS Staff
   Paul F. Nora, MD, FACS, Chicago

LIST OF CONTRIBUTORS

W. Eugene Basanta, JD, LLM
Associate Dean and Associate
 Professor
Southern Illinois University
 School of Law
Carbondale, IL
II/Current Medical-Legal Concepts

Sara C. Charles, MD
Professor of Clinical Psychiatry
Department of Psychiatry
University of Illinois at Chicago
Chicago
*VI/The Complaint, During the
Process, After the Litigation Is
Resolved*

Alfred J. Clementi, MD, FACS
Private Practice
Northwest Surgical Associates
Arlington Heights, IL
Director
Illinois State Inter-Insurance
 Service
III/Risk Financing

John E. Connolly, MD, FACS
Professor of Surgery
University of California, Irvine
Irvine, CA
IV/Office and Outpatient Settings

Joseph B. Davis, MD, FACS
Private Practice
Davis Clinic
Marion, IN
IV/Surgeon-Patient Relationship

M. Martin Halley, MD, JD, FACS
Private Practice
Thoracic and Cardiovascular
 Surgery
Executive Director
Midwest Institute for Health Care
 and Law
Associate Clinical Professor
University of Kansas Health
 Science Center
Topeka, KS
*II/Efforts to Reform and Change;
V/Surgeon-Attorney Relationship,
The Deposition, The Trial, Settle-
ment, Protecting One's Assets*

Kenneth V. Heland, JD
Associate Director
Department of Professional
 Liability
American College of Obstetricians
 and Gynecologists
Washington, DC
IV/The Resident

PROFESSIONAL LIABILITY/RISK MANAGEMENT – A MANUAL FOR SURGEONS

CHARLES A. HERBST, JR., MD, FACS
Professor of Surgery
University of North Carolina at Chapel Hill
School of Medicine
Chapel Hill, NC
IV/Departments of Surgery

WILLIAM W. KRIDELBAUGH, MD, FACS
Private Practice
Clinical Professor of Surgery
University of New Mexico
College of Medicine
Albuquerque
IV/Surgeon-Patient Relationship

THEODORE R. LE BLANG, JD
Legal Counsel
Southern Illinois University School of Medicine
Springfield, IL
Professor of Medical Jurisprudence
Department of Medical Humanities
Southern Illinois University School of Medicine
Springfield, IL
II/Current Medical-Legal Concepts

GEORGE D. MALKASIAN, JR., MD, FACOG, FACS
Senior Consultant
Department of Obstetrics and Gynecology
Mayo Clinic
Professor
Mayo Medical School
Rochester, MN
IV/The Resident

BARRY M. MANUEL, MD, FACS
Associate Dean
Professor of Surgery
Boston University School of Medicine
Boston
II/Efforts to Reform and Change

IAN NISONSON, MD, FACS
Active Staff - Urology
Baptist Hospital of Miami
South Miami Hospital
Clinical Assistant Professor
University of Miami School of Medicine
Department of Urology
Miami
IV/Proper Documentation—The Medical Record

PAUL F. NORA, MD, FACS
Director
Professional Liability Program
American College of Surgeons
Chicago
Professor of Clinical Surgery
Northwestern University Medical School
Chicago
Chairman
Department of Surgery
Columbus Hospital
Chicago
Editor; I/Background and Introduction to the Manual

DONALD J. PALMISANO, MD, JD, FACS
Clinical Professor of Surgery
Clinical Professor of Medical Jurisprudence
Tulane University School of Medicine
New Orleans
President
The Medical Risk Manager Company
Metairie, LA
IV/Consent and the Process of Informed Consent

List Of Contributors

ANDREW H. PATTERSON, MD, FACS
Director of Orthopaedic Surgery
St. Luke's-Roosevelt Hospital
 Center
New York City
President
Medical Liability Mutual
 Insurance Company
New York City
III/Risk Financing

RICHARD L. ROVIT, MD, MSc, FACS
Chairman
Department of Neurological
 Surgery
St. Vincent's Hospital and Medical
 Center of New York
New York City
Professor of Clinical Neurosurgery
New York University School of
 Medicine
New York City
*V/Surgeon-Attorney Relationship,
The Deposition, The Trial*

DAVID C. SABISTON, JR., MD, FACS
James B. Duke Professor and
 Chairman
Department of Surgery
Duke University Medical Center
Durham, NC
II/Historical Review

FRANK C. SPENCER, MD, FACS
Professor and Chairman
Department of Surgery
New York University Medical
 Center
New York City
Chairman
Professional Liability Committee
American College of Surgeons
Chicago
*V/Surgeon-Attorney Relationship,
The Deposition, The Trial*

KEITH C. WHITE, MD, FACOG
Director
Fellowship Activities
American College of Obstetricians
 and Gynecologists
Washington, DC
IV/The Resident

ACKNOWLEDGMENTS

Sincere appreciation is extended to all of the people who helped with the content and production of this manual. Specifically, we would like to acknowledge the following individuals, who have provided reviews, research, guidance, and advice:

General—Martin J. Hatlie, JD, director, Department of Professional Liability and Insurance, American Medical Association, Chicago; and Jeffrey O'Connell, JD, Samuel H. McCoy II professor of law, University of Virginia (Charlottesville) School of Law, Charlottesville. **Chapter I**—C. Rollins Hanlon, MD, FACS, executive consultant, American College of Surgeons. **Chapter II**—Marsha Ryan, MD, JD, FACS, adjunct professor of law, Southern Illinois University, and general surgeon in private practice, Carbondale, IL; Wayne T. Stratton, Esquire, Goodell, Stratton, Edmonds and Palmer, Topeka, KS; and Susan E. Tedrick, law student, Southern Illinois University School of Law, Carbondale. **Chapters III and IV**—James F. Holzer, JD, chief executive officer, Ophthalmic Mutual Insurance Company, San Francisco. **Chapter V**—The Honorable William D. Maddux, Circuit Court judge, Law Division, Chicago; and The Honorable James A. Pusateri, U.S. Bankruptcy Court, Topeka, KS. **Glossary**—Douglas Danner, JD, Powers & Hall, Professional Corporation, Boston; and Ilene Davidson Johnson, JD, staff attorney, Department of Professional Liability and Insurance, American Medical Association, Chicago.

Recognition also should be given to the following members of the staff of the American College of Surgeons for their efforts in coordinating the project and producing this manual: Eleanor Alberstadt, administrative assistant, Professional Liability Program; Donna Pruzin, desktop specialist, Communications Department; Tanisse Bezin, general publications manager, Communications Department; and Linn Meyer, director, Communications Department.

PAUL F. NORA, MD, FACS

I / BACKGROUND AND INTRODUCTION TO THE MANUAL

Background

The American College of Surgeons has long had an interest in professional liability. When the medical malpractice litigation crisis of the early 1970s occurred because of changes in the nature of available liability insurance and the inability of some surgeons to secure essential coverage, the College's interest in this problem intensified. College officials were stimulated to discuss these concerns with the National Association of Insurance Commissioners in 1973.

At that time, the College also conducted an extensive investigation into the possibility of developing a professional liability insurance program for its own Fellows. However, numerous obstacles, such as the variable requirements of state insurance regulators, militated against the College's role as a national underwriter of professional liability insurance.

Nonetheless, the College's interest in issues related to professional liability remained intense. Consistent with its role as an educational organization, the College introduced the first edition of its *Patient Safety Manual* in 1974, followed by the publication of *Providing Management Information for Patient Safety Programs* in 1980 and the second edition of the *Patient Safety Manual* in 1985.

The Ad Hoc Regental Committee on Professional Liability of the 1970s was the *main impetus* behind the College's professional liability activities, and in 1985, it became a permanent, special committee of the Regents. Criteria for the composition of the membership of this committee include special expertise in professional liability issues, and specialty and geographic representation.

As one of its many charges, the Professional Liability Committee responds to the concerns of the Fellows with regard to professional liability problems and issues. Each year since 1978, the Governors of the College have submitted reports on the attitudes and concerns of Fellows in their geographic or specialty areas, and as evidenced by these reports, professional liability has maintained a top-priority status among the Fellowship. Over the years, the members of the committee have responded to Fellows' concerns by authoring articles, sponsoring postgraduate courses, and participating in ACS panel discussions dealing with various aspects of the professional liability issue. In addition, the committee has encouraged and supported the College's active participation in the AMA/Specialty Society Medical Liability Project, which is working to develop an alternative to the current system of resolving medical liability disputes.

Introduction

Recently, in the course of their discussions, the members of the Professional Liability Committee perceived a need to develop a manual on professional liability *for surgeons*. Recognizing the difficulty of setting down a definitive, comprehensive solution to this multifaceted problem, the members of the committee deemed it nevertheless desirable to publish a basic reference manual in the area of professional liability and risk management. Thus, this manual was written for the purpose of providing the practicing surgeon with an up-to-date reference that has as its main thrust to present in a clear, concise manner the nature of the law as it applies today in the area of medical torts. Repetition in certain areas that call for special emphasis is purposeful.

I / Introduction and Background

First, the reader will find a brief history of the law, followed by a review of substantive, pertinent legal principles and a discussion of possible future directions.

Attention is then turned to the topic of risk management as it applies to surgeons. As currently defined, risk management is a systematic approach to identifying, evaluating, reducing, or eliminating risk due to an undesirable deviation from an anticipated outcome, thereby preventing the loss of financial assets resulting from injury to patients. Thus, in this manual, the topic is divided into three functions: (1) risk financing (insurance), (2) risk prevention, and (3) loss control. It should be noted that these three aspects of risk management may take place concurrently.

In the discussion of risk financing, the reader is provided with data that can be used in making reasonable decisions about appropriate types of insurance coverage.

The cornerstone of risk prevention is the *competence* of the surgeon, both intellectually and technically. This competence is based on education, training, and experience. The importance of competence is implied in any discussion of risk prevention. Because surgical competence is the focus of so many of the College's programs and activities, it is not included as a part of the subject matter that is discussed in the section on risk prevention in this text.

The discussion of risk prevention clarifies for the surgeon the many areas in which appropriate strategies may negate or lessen the likelihood of adverse legal action, which may be either factual or unfounded. Although the importance of maintaining solid and amiable physician-patient relationships is emphasized, the need to have adequate documentation is stressed. The section on risk prevention covers special situations for the reader, such as those that occur in the office, in the ambulatory surgery facility, or in the department of surgery. In addition, special problems faced by residents are addressed, and the process of informed consent is thoroughly explored.

Loss control is that function that attempts to minimize liability following an adverse occurrence to a patient. Loss control can be divided chronologically into incident management and claims management. Incident management relies heavily on two areas that are discussed in the risk prevention chapter—namely, the importance of good surgeon-patient communications and the need to have adequate documentation. These two areas become even more important if an adverse event occurs.

Because the appropriate approach to incident management is well described in the *Litigation Assistant*, a pamphlet that was published by the American College of Obstetricians and Gynecologists in 1986 and reprinted by the American College of Surgeons in May 1987, it is not included in this manual. However, the manual brings the claims management function into focus. This function relies heavily on the surgeon-attorney relationship, and occurs if the patient files a claim at a later date.

Claims management refers to the appropriate activities that should be undertaken after a legal claim has been filed by a patient following an adverse event, whether real or perceived. Thus, as a major part of loss control, claims management is described in detail in this book. A review of interrogatories, depositions, and preparation for and behavior during trial are provided. The role of the plaintiff expert witness and methods for dealing with inappropriate testimony at a trial are included. The options of settlement and appeal are described, and protection of the defendant's assets is also addressed.

Finally, the psychological trauma of the litigation process to both surgeon and patient are elaborated upon in a realistic, but humane, fashion.

The members of the Professional Liability Committee of the American College of Surgeons hope that this manual will provide significant guidance for surgeons in an era when so many adverse factors have come together to obstruct their primary goal of providing optimal patient care.

II / SUBSTANTIVE TORT LAW

Editor's Note

Substantive tort law as it applies to medical malpractice has evolved from the early beginnings of English common law to the time of the litigation explosion that occurred in the 1970s and beyond. This initial section provides a discussion of the history and evolution of medical malpractice law.

The major legal elements that are necessary to prove medical malpractice are described in detail. Appropriate examples of what is required for each of the specific elements are named, and citations reported from various jurisdictions are described.

The various types of damages and how they are assessed are detailed, with appropriate case examples. A description of contract law as it applies to medical torts is given.

An understanding of the agency relationship as it relates to the surgeons incurring liability for the acts of others is thoroughly discussed with descriptive examples. The concepts of the Borrowed Servant and the Captain of the Ship doctrine as it applies to surgeons are presented. The importance of certain statutory immunities to encourage physician involvement in patient care and peer review without incurring liability are emphasized.

Several types of legal defenses in cases of medical malpractice are listed. Specifically, compliance of surgeons to adherence to a reasonable standard of care, appropriate determination of statutes of limitation, and the possibility of patient negligence as useful defenses are described.

In the final section, various types of tort reform that have been attempted or enacted are presented. The importance of caps on awards, particularly for noneconomic damages, modification of collateral source rule, and shorten-

ing of statutes of limitation are mentioned as the most effective reforms to reduce frequency and severity of claims.

An overhaul of the present tort system is strongly recommended. Several methods of alternative dispute resolutions (ADR) are described in detail. Specifically, the fault-based alternative, contractual approach, early offer and recovery, and the no-fault patient compensation model are presented with both advantages and disadvantages. The negative effects on the physician-patient relationship of our existing tort system mandates a major change.

Historical Review

The Code of Hammurabi is generally regarded as the first codification of law to cite the issue of clinical malpractice. Later, the Greek philosopher Plato held that the actions of physicians should be judged *solely* by other physicians, believing they were best able to render knowledgeable decisions. Aristotle believed that the only penalty applicable to wrongdoing by a physician, either real or perceived, was injury to the physician's reputation.

American malpractice laws have their ancestral origin in the common law of Anglo-Saxon England. From the time of the Norman Conquest in 1066, the common law was a flexible system that could be adapted to specific situations. In this way, it contrasted with the more definitive and fixed interpretations of Roman law. Therefore, in common law, when a situation arose for which no precedent had been established, the judiciary had authority to decide freely.

The first civil liability suit recorded in English law was brought before the King's Bench in 1374. The defendant, J. Mort, a surgeon, was sued by a patient who had sustained a hand injury. The defendant was found not liable, because of a legal technicality, but the court ruled that if negligence could be proved in such a situation, the law would provide a remedy. Interestingly, the court added another comment, stating, "If the surgeon does so well as he can and employs all his diligence to the cure, it is not right that he should be held culpable." Interesting, too, is the fact that surgical professional liability insurance was available even then in the form of a renewable "floater" policy, which required mandatory consultation on any high-risk case.

In 1423, the Joint College of Physicians and Surgeons of London drafted the "Ordinance Against Malpractice," which was written in English rather than in Latin or French, the classical legal languages of the period. It stipulated that a surgeon must report all desperately ill patients within three days of examining them. When the College of Physicians of London was incorporated in 1518, its charter provided that the college could initiate action against its members for malpractice, which was punishable by a fine of £60 or 13 days of imprisonment. Many of the plea records of that era are still available and have served as evidence in subsequent suits. In fact, the doctrine of *stare decisis*—that is, a judgment based upon a previous decision—in its adherence to precedent remains the most significant feature of English common law.

Initially, criminal and tort law coincided, and some overlap between these two areas of the law continues today. While criminal law demands punishment and deterrence of criminals in the interest of public security, tort liability for "private crimes" seeks to appease the victims of crimes, discouraging personal retaliation by providing for payment of damages. Tort law originally was concerned with causation—that is, whether an injury was direct or indirect—rather than with "moral" considerations regarding intent or careless behavior.

In later centuries, criminal and tort law gradually diverged, although the same act could still constitute both a crime and a tort. With the industrial revolution came profound changes in society, including rapid population growth and a more densely concentrated population, more accidents, and a multitude of other inevitable results of the increasing opportunity for human interaction. As "the pulse of human activity" accelerated, so did the development of tort law, which expanded its limits, recognized new concepts, and established new and sometimes even nameless torts. Intent and carelessness became more important considerations in determining fault, and a hypothetical "prudent man" was established as the standard for determining unreasonable behavior. By the end of the 19th century, contemporary legal theory was reflected in the slogan "no liability without fault."

In the United States, the first medical liability suit was filed in 1794. In that suit, *Cross v. Guthrey*, Dr. Guthrey, a surgeon, was sued by a patient's husband, who charged him with guilt and negligence in the performance of a mastectomy, alleging that his wife had been operated on "in the most unskillful, ignorant and cruel manner contrary to all the well-known rules and principles of practice in such cases, that the patient survived by but three hours, and that the defendant had wholly broken and violated his undertaking and promise to the plaintiff to perform said operation skillfully and with safety to this wife." The jury found the physician liable and awarded damages of $140.

As time has passed and the number of medical malpractice cases in the United States increased, more recent decisions by judges and juries have greatly expanded the earlier concepts of precedence, resulting in extremely large settlements. As a result, it is now apparent that a new pattern of judicial review exists that is unlike its English counterpart in many ways.

The concept that negligence constitutes a tort in itself developed during the mid-19th century to become an important concept in tort law. Until then, negligence had played only an ancillary role in other tort actions, especially those involving individuals such as innkeepers, mail carriers, pharmacists, attorneys, blacksmiths, and surgeons, whose occupations subjected them to a particularly high degree of exposure to the public.

Early records also serve to dramatize the rise in current professional liability suits. In a review of malpractice suits in American medicine from 1794 to 1861, the author could identify only 27 malpractice suits that had been appealed to the various state supreme courts. Even later, in the 20 years from 1935 to 1955, there were only 605 such cases. Since then, however, the number of professional liability suits has skyrocketed and the rocket has yet to return to earth, making the current era a very troublesome one, indeed, for the medical profession.

Beginning in the early 1970s, there was a precipitous rise in the filing of medical malpractice claims in the United States, which resulted in a marked increase of payments for the plaintiff. The cause of increased suits, with the high indemnity payments, is probably the result of many factors. A partial list of these factors includes changes in the physician-patient relationship, technology, and expectations of patients; liberal pro plaintiff judiciary; a lack of understanding by the juries; and a pro active plaintiff bar.

In 1973, a report of the Secretary's Commission from the U.S. Department of Health and Human Services on medical malpractice was published to assess these marked changes that were occurring. During this period, the healthcare provider insurers withdrew in certain geographic areas, and, concurrently, there was an increase in the premiums and, frequently, modification in their type of coverage. This initial crisis peaked in 1975. There was also decreased availability of medical care in several states, such as California, New York, Florida, and Illinois.

Subsequently, many states passed legislation—sometimes ill conceived—to ameliorate the distortion by the tort system. Many of these tort reforms were subsequently attacked on the grounds of lack of constitutionality. Many of these hard-fought tort reforms were overturned by the state supreme court. The federal government had not sought to involve itself in preemptive tort reform. Most of these tort reforms were at the state level; however, at this time, some progress was made in stabilizing the increase in insurance premiums.

Although easing of the crisis occurred (namely, decrease in the cost of medical malpractice insurance), it was short lived. Insurance premiums continued to escalate,

II / Substantive Tort Law

and liability in other areas became more manifest. From a medical malpractice standpoint, a major part of the new crisis in the mid-1980s was the affordability of insurance coverage and the need for excess insurance to cover the much higher settlements. The changing emphasis toward comparative negligence, with its effect on joint and several liability, was also felt. Subsequently, the need for achieving tort reform that could withstand constitutional muster became more obvious. Certain states, such as California and Indiana, were quite effective in tort reform activity by modifying certain elements, such as creating caps on economic loss and collateral source offset. Meanwhile, legislation passed in other states, such as Florida and Texas, was then struck down by the state supreme court on a constitutional basis. In the last ten to 15 years, many reforms dealing with this crisis have been brought forward and will be discussed in the "Efforts to Reform and Change" section of the present chapter.

Current Medical-Legal Concepts

The medical malpractice climate in the United States today makes it imperative that surgeons be aware of the medical-legal environment within which the adjudication of malpractice liability occurs and of their rights and responsibilities in the physician-patient relationship.

The Surgeon-Patient Relationship

Under the law, a surgeon has no obligation to accept or treat every patient who seeks surgical care and treatment. Rather, the surgeon-patient relationship is consensual in nature, coming into being only when a patient requests treatment and a surgeon agrees to provide it, or when a surgeon agrees to treat a patient on the basis of a referral. Once the relationship exists, however, the surgeon is obligated to employ skill, care, and knowledge in the performance of his or her professional duties. Whether or not the surgeon-patient relationship does in fact exist can in itself become a legal issue.

For example, in *Davis v. Weiskopf*, 439 N.E.2d 60 (Ill. App. 1982), the court was asked to consider whether a physician-patient relationship existed under facts alleged by the patient in his complaint.

This section was adapted in part from LeBlang TR, Basanta WE (credits also given to Peters J, Fineberg K, Kroll D): The Law of Medical Practice in Illinois. *Lawyers Cooperative Publishing Company, 1986.*

According to the allegations in *Davis*, the patient's knee had been x-rayed in a hospital emergency room, showing a giant cell lesion. Without advising the patient of his observations, the treating physician consulted with a specialist, the defendant in the case, and referred the patient to him for treatment. The patient's initial appointment was rescheduled by the specialist before he saw the patient. When the patient called about the rescheduled appointment, he allegedly was told that the defendant would not treat him. The patient later claimed he was neither told of the lesion by the specialist nor referred to another physician. Because the lesion was cancerous, the patient's leg eventually was amputated, as a result of which the suit was brought.

The trial court dismissed the patient's complaint against the specialist, finding that, as a matter of law, no physician-patient relationship existed under the circumstances. However, an appellate court reversed that decision, holding that, under the facts presented in the complaint, the defendant had a duty to the patient. The court observed that the defendant had allegedly accepted referral of the case and knew that the patient might have a malignancy of the knee, and that the patient's subsequent medical problems were reasonably foreseeable under those circumstances. The defendant could easily have discharged his duties, the court suggested, by advising the patient of his condition and of the need to consult with another physician promptly.

Terminating the Relationship

As a general principle of law, once the surgeon-patient relationship has been established, the surgeon is obligated to provide all appropriate care to the patient as long as the patient's condition requires it. Thus, courts typically have concluded that the relationship cannot be terminated at will by the surgeon, but must continue throughout the period during which treatment is necessary, or until the relationship is concluded either by mutual consent of the parties or for another legally acceptable reason. A surgeon's failure to adequately provide for a patient's continuing welfare while medical or surgical attention is required could result in a malpractice claim based on a breach of professional standards or abandonment.

Longman v. Jasiek, 414 N.E.2d 520 (Ill. App. 1980), is one such case in which the failure of the defendant, an oral surgeon, to continue to provide necessary care and treatment to the patient was found to constitute abandonment.

The *Longman* suit arose after the oral surgeon extracted several of the patient's wisdom teeth. A few days later, after the sutures were removed, the patient experienced pain, stiffness, and swelling in her jaw, and contacted the oral surgeon. Because the pain was not in the area of the jaw where the teeth had been removed, the oral surgeon told the patient that her problems were not related to the surgical operation and advised her to contact her family physician. The family physician prescribed a modest dosage of oral penicillin.

While this treatment provided some temporary relief, intense pain and stiffness returned within a few days. Again contacting the oral surgeon, the patient was once more instructed to see her family physician, who again prescribed penicillin. When the patient's condition persisted, she was admitted by the family physician to a hospital, where osteomyelitis was eventually diagnosed.

In her suit against the oral surgeon, the patient claimed that "as a result of his abandonment and refusal to treat [her], an abscess developed in the right part of her jaw which eventually reached the bone and developed into osteomyelitis." On appeal, the reviewing court concluded that the evidence was sufficient to support the jury's verdict that the oral surgeon had abandoned the patient and that such abandonment had proximately caused the patient's osteomyelitis.

As *Longman* indicates, a surgeon has a duty to provide treatment to a patient for as long as the patient's condition requires it. However, despite the clear obligations of a surgeon to provide for the on-going care of a patient in accordance with established professional standards, there are circumstances in which a surgeon-patient relationship may legally be terminated. For example, the relationship may legally be terminated when the patient's care is fully transferred to another surgeon, when the patient no longer requires surgical or related follow-up care, when the contract or understanding between the surgeon and the patient specifically limits the treatment that the surgeon is obligated to provide (as, for example, when the surgeon's only responsibility to the patient is to perform a disability evaluation), or when the surgeon is discharged at the specific direction of the patient.

The relationship may also be legally terminated when the surgeon withdraws from it after providing adequate written notification. In that event, however, it is essential to provide the patient with adequate written notice that includes a statement of the reasons for terminating the relationship, as well as enough time to enable the patient to obtain future care elsewhere.

Medical Malpractice Tort Claims

Today, most medical malpractice actions in the United States that involve surgical care and treatment are based on the legal principles of tort law or negligence. A tort is defined as a civil wrong, other than a breach of contract, for which the law provides a remedy in the form of monetary damages. The primary basis for tort liability in medical malpractice is negligence, which may be described as an act or omission that deviates from what a reasonably prudent person would or would not do in a similar situation.

In assessing a medical malpractice tort claim, the courts measure a physician's conduct against what a "reasonably prudent" medical practitioner would have done in the same or similar circumstances. Thus, surgical malpractice could appropriately be characterized as an act or omission that constitutes a breach of the surgeon's obligation to employ reasonable skill and care in the treatment of a patient.

To recover damages from a surgeon on the basis of malpractice, a patient must prove four things: (1) that the surgeon owed the patient a particular duty to act in conformity with certain patient care norms or standards that have been established by the profession, (2) that an act or omission on the part of the surgeon violated those established norms or standards of care, (3) that there was a causal connection between the act or omission of the surgeon and a resulting injury to the patient, and (4) that the patient suffered actual loss or damage as a result of that injury.

In litigating a medical malpractice claim, a patient bears the burden of proving each of these elements by a preponderance of the evidence. In other words, the patient must prove that it is more probably true than not that the surgeon owed a duty to the patient and that that duty was breached, proximately causing injury that resulted in loss or damage to the patient.

The Standard of Care

As a general principle of law, a surgeon must possess and apply the knowledge, skill, and care ordinarily used by reasonably well-qualified surgeons practicing in similar cases and circumstances. These obligations are referred to as adhering to the *standard of care*. In some states, and under some circumstances, courts may measure the practice of reasonably well-qualified surgeons against the practices that are applicable in the same or in similar localities. This measure of conduct is referred to as the *locality rule*.

The locality rule developed in the United States in the 1800s to protect rural practitioners, who were then viewed as having less access to educational resources, equipment, and facilities than were available to their colleagues practicing in urban areas. Since then, as communications, transportation, and access to technological advances have improved, many states have abandoned the rule. This is especially true in relation to cases involving physicians who hold themselves out to the public as specialists in their field. Thus, it is not unusual for courts to conclude that specialists should be held to a nationally articulated standard of care, based on the fact that geographic conditions typically have less impact on specialty practice and that specialists often are members of organizations that publish nationally applicable criteria for training and certification.

While courts are thus inclined to hold that a specialist's practice locality or community is national in scope, this view may be less appropriate in cases that raise the issue of whether a rural specialist had access to medical technology that is available only in urban centers. However, in reviewing cases that focus on such considerations as the method of treatment or kind of surgical technique used, the courts are most likely to conclude that nationally articulated standards constitute the most appropriate measure of due care, wherever it is provided.

The nature of a particular patient's medical problem and the circumstances in which it is encountered will, of course, have a significant bearing on the standard of care that the courts are likely to apply in considering a given treatment situation. While it is obviously beyond the scope of this discussion to detail all the treatment procedures and disease entities that may be involved in malpractice actions, it may nonetheless be useful to discuss several such situations to illustrate how the standard of care concept may be applied. It should be emphasized that the issues of consent and informed consent to treatment are discussed thoroughly in Chapter IV and, thus, are not addressed in this chapter.

Diagnosis Surgeons are obligated to follow established standards of practice in diagnosing the causes of illness. Among other things, these standards include taking a proper medical history, conducting an adequate physical examination, properly utilizing laboratory and ancillary procedures, and reasonably evaluating available information in making a diagnosis.

As a general rule, surgeons are not held liable for diagnostic mistakes made when a patient's symptoms are unusual or obscure, or when the patient's condition is susceptible to varied or multiple interpretations. However, a surgeon could be held liable for mistakes made as a result of failure to conduct an adequate examination, and the surgeon's utilization of available scientific information and diagnostic tools is likely to be considered in determining the adequacy of an examination.

The case of *Wheat v. United States*, 630 F. Supp. 699 (W.D. Tex. 1986), provides one example of a failure to conform to the standard of care in making an accurate diagnosis.

The patient in *Wheat* was a 37-year-old woman who, after taking birth control pills for six years, sought treatment at a military hospital in May 1978 for severe menstrual cramps, heavy menstrual bleeding, a painful pelvis, painful intercourse, and an unusual, white jelly-like discharge. A Pap smear taken at the time revealed minimal dysplasia; no other diagnostic tests were performed. Two months later, when the patient's problems persisted, an endometrial biopsy of the upper part of the uterus was performed, but proved negative. Neither fractional dilation and curettage (D&C) nor a laparoscopy were performed, and no further tests were ordered at this time. Although a fractional D&C and laparoscopy were subsequently ordered, they were not performed because the patient's husband was transferred. The patient did return to her military physicians a few months later; however, these procedures were never again ordered.

Over the next several years, the patient's pain and problems intensified. A private physician performed a hysterectomy on the patient in 1979, at which time a report of pathologic findings revealed a stage IIB cancer of the cervix. However, the private physician told neither the patient nor her family of this fact and never treated her cancer. Nor was her cancer diagnosed in 1980, when the patient again saw her military physicians, who did not seek to obtain the patient's medical records from her private physician. Furthermore, no diagnostic tests or biopsy were performed, despite the presence of several signs of cancer, including an abnormal mass at the cuff of the vagina and an ovary that was firm and fixed. Instead, when the patient's pain persisted, pain medication was prescribed and the patient was told that her problems were psychological rather than physiological.

Despite continued visits to her military physicians, the patient's cancer remained undiagnosed, and her condition deteriorated. Finally, in March 1981, the patient suffered renal failure because of cancer in the pelvis and was admitted to the hospital in a comatose condition. There, her cervical cancer, now terminal, was diagnosed. The patient died in March 1982.

In the malpractice action initiated by the patient's family against the United States and the private physician, the federal district court observed that, "[t]he record in this case is replete with evidence of the failure of the Army physicians to perform the appropriate diagnostic tests," such as a Pap smear, biopsy, or laparoscopy. The court held that the standard of proper medical care required that these tests be performed and that, if they had been, the patient's cancer would have been detected, and proper treatment could have been provided. Thus, the court ruled, the failure to perform these diagnostic tests was a proximate cause of the patient's pain, suffering, and untimely wrongful death.

As *Wheat* indicates, the importance of making an accurate diagnosis based upon available data and utilization of proper diagnostic tools cannot be overemphasized. Nevertheless, a surgeon is not obligated to render a flawless performance.

In *Bush v. United States*, 703 F.2d 491 (11th Cir. 1983), for example, the court concluded that a surgeon's failure to make an accurate diagnosis did not constitute medical malpractice.

Bush involved a claim against the United States for the alleged negligence of Veterans Administration Hospital physicians in misdiagnosing a patient's condition as pancreatic cancer. The patient had been admitted to the hospital after experiencing loss of appetite, nausea, jaundice, and excretion of dark urine for several days. Although extensive tests indicated obstructive jaundice, some diagnostic data suggested pancreatic cancer. Exploratory operation was performed, during which a stone obstructing the common duct was removed. The surgeon, uncertain as to whether he had in fact located the true source of the patient's problem, conducted seven biopsies of the pancreas, the results of all of which were negative. However, a cholangiogram showed the biliary ducts to be dilated, and the head of the patient's pancreas felt enlarged and grainy.

Consistent with treatment policies of the hospital staff, the surgeon proceeded to perform a Whipple procedure. Immediately after surgical operation, the patient began to bleed and went into shock, remaining hospitalized until he died six weeks later. Clinical evidence later indicated that the patient in fact did not have cancer.

An action brought by the patient's widow claimed negligence in the performance of unnecessary surgical operation based on the misdiagnosis of cancer. At trial, expert witnesses presented conflicting testimony as to the appropriateness of the surgical procedure under the circumstances. The defense expert stated that, while he might not have made the same choice, the election to proceed with the Whipple procedure was a "judgment decision."

The court of appeals upheld a district court ruling that there had been no medical malpractice in the situation, observing that the evidence showed that the physicians were faced with a difficult decision based on conflicting diagnostic information. Under those circumstances, the court ruled, "it cannot be said that the V.A. surgeons deviated from acceptable medical practices. Their decision to proceed with the Whipple procedure did not violate the standard of care customarily followed in this particular type of case, according to those who are qualified to perform similar services in the community."

Thus, it should be clear that, while a surgeon is expected to possess and apply the knowledge and use the skill and care that would ordinarily be used by reasonably well-qualified surgeons in diagnosing a patient's condition, this standard of care does not require the surgeon to render a perfect performance or to be a guarantor of a diagnosis.

Care and Treatment The surgeon also has the responsibility of possessing and applying the knowledge and using the skill and care that ordinarily would be used by reasonably well-qualified surgeons in the care and treatment of patients.

This obligation is demonstrated by *McCord v. Maguire*, 873 F.2d 1271 (9th Cir. 1989), in which a surgeon's failure to conform to the standard of care in performing gallbladder operation resulted in a substantial damage award.

During the surgical operation at issue in *McCord*, the defendant surgeon had performed a cholangiogram to determine whether the patient's common bile duct was obstructed by a stone. The surgeon initially misplaced the catheter and had to retract it. He then injected 25 cc of dye into the bile duct. When a review of the X rays indicated what the surgeon thought to be a stone, he proceeded with exploratory surgery of the duct. No stones were found, however, and the patient was discharged from the hospital several days later.

A month later, the patient came to the hospital emergency room experiencing abdominal pain and gastrointestinal bleeding. An examination by the defendant surgeon revealed complete blockage of the patient's common bile duct and hemobilia. The defendant again performed exploratory surgery rather than attempting embolization and found both bleeding into the patient's bile duct and an apparent occlusion of the hepatic artery. The patient was given heparin. Although continuation of the exploratory surgery resulted in destruction of the common bile duct, the source of the bleeding was determined to be a fistula from the common bile duct to the gastroduodenal artery. The surgeon stopped the bleeding by tying off the artery, but was unable to repair the common bile duct.

Following the surgical operation, the patient continued to bleed and was transferred to another hospital, where she was admitted with adult respiratory distress syndrome, congestive heart failure, and kidney failure, as well as both a bile duct disruption and hepatic ischemia.

The patient subsequently filed suit against the surgeon, alleging multiple acts of negligence and seeking to demonstrate failure on the part of the surgeon to exercise due care in her treatment. The trial judge submitted the case to a jury, instructing the jurors that the patient had the burden of proving, by a preponderance of the evidence, that the defendant was negligent and that such negligence had caused the patient's injuries and damages. The jury returned a verdict for the patient in the amount of $1.8 million. An appellate court upheld the verdict, despite the defendant's claim that certain alleged acts of negligence were not supported by the evidence, finding instead "substantial evidence to support both the jury's finding of medical negligence and its award of damages." Accordingly, the $1.8 million verdict in favor of the patient was allowed to stand.

Follow-up Care The obligation to conform to the standard of care in performing an operation or surgical procedure is complemented by the surgeon's duty to provide adequate follow-up care. Among other things, the surgeon is obligated to appropriately monitor a patient's condition and respond in a timely fashion to evident complications.

The case of *Momsen v. Nebraska Methodist Hospital*, 313 N.W.2d 208 (Neb. 1981), exemplifies a finding of surgical negligence as a result of failure to adequately care for a patient in the face of postoperative complications.

In *Momsen*, the defendant surgeon had performed a hysterectomy on a patient who was generally in good health. Several hours after the surgical operation, the patient began showing signs of distress. A nurse noted that the patient's breathing was "very moist" and that it was necessary to suction fluid from the patient's throat at various times throughout the evening. In addition, the patient's pulse rate had risen and her blood pressure fallen. When the nurse observed that the patient's fingernails were cyanotic, she contacted the surgeon, who was at home, and advised him of the patient's status. Believing a hemorrhage to be the probable cause of the problems, the surgeon ordered a hematocrit and directed the nurse to increase intravenous fluids. Later, the nurse again contacted the surgeon to inform him of the results of the hematocrit, which showed no blood loss. The surgeon instructed the nurse to continue to watch the patient closely, but did not return to the hospital to see the patient. When the patient went into cardiac arrest an hour later, resuscitation efforts were unsuccessful and she died early the next day. Autopsy results established pulmonary edema as the cause of death.

The patient's estate brought suit against the surgeon and the hospital. At trial, the jury returned a verdict in favor of both the surgeon and the hospital, but the trial judge granted the estate's motion for a new trial as to the surgeon. On appeal, the central issue was whether, on the basis of the evidence presented, the surgeon's postoperative care was negligent. The Nebraska Supreme Court reviewed the evidence, including extensive expert testimony that the care provided to the patient was inadequate, and concluded that the judge's ruling against the surgeon was proper. The court noted that the defendant "had knowledge of the patient's symptoms and their serious nature. He did not go to the hospital to make a personal examination and attempt further diagnosis. There was nothing to prevent him from so doing. He was negligent as a matter of law in these respects." Thus, under the facts of the case, the surgeon's negligence in failing to promptly and personally attend the patient was viewed by the court as being clear and unambiguous.

Referrals Surgeons are both ethically and legally obligated to refrain from practicing beyond their area of specialized competence. Therefore, surgeons are obligated to refer patients to appropriate subspecialists when their condition warrants it. The clinical indications demanding consultation or referral will, of course, vary from case to case. When a surgeon realizes, or reasonably should realize, however, that the nature of a patient's illness or condition requires the services of a subspecialist, the courts are likely to view the standard of care as requiring that the surgeon advise the patient accordingly.

Failure to refer a case resulted in liability for several physicians in *Haley v. United States*, 739 F.2d 1502 (10th Cir. 1984).

The patient in *Haley* had previously been diagnosed as having Crohn's disease and had had her colon removed and an ileostomy created. Four years later, when she experienced vomiting and abdominal cramps, a biopsy revealed inflammation in the rectal stump. The biopsy specimen was analyzed by one of the several defendant physicians, who, allegedly without reviewing the patient's prior treatment records, concluded that the patient might have either ulcerative colitis or Crohn's disease and that the rectal stump might be cancerous. Two reports of pathologic findings stated that a possible, but uncertain, diagnosis was chronic ulcerative colitis. Thereafter, another of the defendants, the hospital chief of surgery, took the patient's history and performed a physical examination, but did not consult the patient's medical records or reports from her prior operations. The patient was informed that the rectal stump might be cancerous and that its removal, although elective, was recommended.

Following surgical operation to remove the rectal stump, which was performed by a third defendant surgeon, the patient developed abdominal and perineal wound infections. The patient filed a lawsuit, claiming that the physicians' treatment was deficient in several respects. In particular, given their uncertain diagnosis of her condition as ulcerative colitis or Crohn's disease, she alleged that the proper course of treatment would have been to advise her to see a gastroenterologist to obtain a more accurate diagnosis.

The importance of obtaining a proper diagnosis under these circumstances was demonstrated by testimony of the patient's expert witnesses at trial. They stated that, while surgical operation was appropriate for ulcerative colitis, it was generally to be avoided in cases of Crohn's disease because of the risk of postsurgical infection. Referral to a gastroenterologist for a proper diagnosis, they argued, would have confirmed Crohn's disease, and the patient could thus have avoided undergoing inappropriate surgical operation.

The trial court entered a judgment in favor of the patient. The appellate court affirmed the judgment, concluding that in order to obtain the patient's informed consent prior to surgical operation, the defendants had "a duty to advise her that the specialized knowledge of a gastroenterologist could aid in obtaining a more accurate diagnosis." Given the defendant's apparent confusion regarding the patient's condition, the court found that due care required such a referral.

As a general rule of law, a physician who refers a patient to a subspecialist for care and treatment is not liable for malpractice on the part of the subspecialist, but there may be exceptions to this rule if, for example, the referring physician continues to provide treatment to the patient in close coordination or cooperation with the subspecialist. However, if the referring physician is only remotely or indirectly involved in the subspecialist's treatment, liability is not likely.

Once a referral has been made, subspecialists are responsible for responding in a timely and appropriate fashion. The subspecialist is therefore required to assess the patient's condition and render the necessary care and follow-up treatment. Failure to do so may result in liability based on principles of abandonment or a violation of the applicable standard of care.

Unnecessary Surgical Operation

In accordance with the standard of care, a surgeon is obligated to refrain from subjecting a patient to unnecessary surgical operation. Whether or not surgical operation is necessary must, of course, be determined by the exercise of reasonable clinical judgment in accordance with the facts of each case. Nevertheless, certain legal and economic considerations have enhanced the scrutiny to which such clinical decision-making is subjected, especially when it involves a decision to perform a hysterectomy, caesarean section, appendectomy, hemorrhoidectomy, or cataract surgery.

Lawsuits involving unnecessary surgical operation typically are filed when a patient suffers postoperative complications that would not have occurred if the surgical procedure had not been performed.

In one such suit, *Niccoli v. Thompson*, 713 S.W.2d 579 (Mo. App. 1986), the court concluded that unnecessary surgical operation constituted a violation of the standard of care.

The patient in *Niccoli* was a 35-year-old woman who was experiencing urinary incontinence and had a lesion on her clitoris. Following an initial diagnosis of "urinary infection, cystitis," a report of pathologic findings suggested that the patient might have squamous cell carcinoma, and she therefore was referred to a surgeon. After the presence of a "squamous cell carcinoma in situ" was established by biopsy, the surgeon consulted with an oncologist, who recommended a "wide simple vulvectomy with excision of the clitoris." However, the patient was told only that she needed some "corrective surgery" to "fix her bladder." Neither physician informed the patient that a vulvectomy would be performed or that there were available other, less radical and disfiguring treatment choices. Following the surgical operation, the patient experienced intense and continuous pain, was unable to engage in sexual intercourse, and suffered from severe emotional problems associated with the surgical operation.

The court found substantial evidence to support the patient's claim that the surgeon was negligent in performing an unnecessary vulvectomy when alternative treatments were available. The court further found that the patient's claim against the oncologist for negligence in recommending the unnecessary surgical operation had been properly submitted to the jury. Given the evidence presented by the patient at trial, an appellate court upheld the decision of the trial judge to grant the patient a new trial following a jury verdict for the oncologist and an inordinately low damage award against the surgeon.

In determining whether a particular surgical operation was necessary, the courts rely on criteria set forth by experts who are familiar with the standard of care in similar circumstances. As the *Bush* case indicated above, a surgeon is not likely to be deemed to have violated the standard of care simply because a diagnosis based on pathologic findings of removed tissue results in postsurgical findings that do not correlate with the original indications for that surgical operation. Finding a physician liable would require demonstrating that his or her decision to operate was contrary to the decision that would have been made by a reasonably well-qualified surgeon practicing under the same or similar circumstances and in light of the available diagnostic information. Clinical decision-making is not, after all, a precise science. Recognizing that, the legal system does not require a surgeon to conform to a standard of care enhanced by the clarity of hindsight.

Breach of Duty

As we have seen, proving medical malpractice requires a patient to establish that a specific standard of care was applicable and to provide evidence that a surgeon deviated from that standard, thus causing the patient's injuries. As a general rule, proof of a violation of the standard of care is established through expert testimony.

Expert testimony is required in medical malpractice litigation because lay jurors are not presumed to be capable of evaluating whether a surgeon has adhered to the proper standard of surgical care and treatment. Accordingly, to determine whether there has been a violation of the standard of care, jurors must rely on evidence offered by surgeons who testify as expert witnesses.

The plaintiff in a medical malpractice action is required to present the jury with expert testimony setting forth the standard of care that applies to the defendant surgeon's conduct, as well as expert testimony indicating that the surgeon breached that standard. In most cases, the expert witness must have qualifications similar to those of the defendant surgeon and be familiar with the applicable standard of care. Whether an expert witness is qualified to testify in a medical malpractice case is a matter that generally is left to the trial judge to determine.

In one case, *Weekly v. Solomon*, 510 N.E.2d 152 (Ill. App. 1987), the court was unwilling to accept the testimony of the patient's expert on the basis of an evident lack of qualifications.

The patient in *Weekly* had undergone a gastric stapling procedure, but failed to lose weight postoperatively. Suing the surgeon, she alleged negligent failure to warn her of the nature and risks of the procedure, failure to prescribe a postoperative weight loss diet, and use of an improper surgical technique.

The patient's surgical operation was performed in Waukegan, Illinois. As her expert witness, she called a general surgeon who practiced in Toledo, Ohio, and had performed gastric stapling procedures, including the Pace method utilized by the defendant surgeon. However, the expert had consulted neither physicians practicing in the Waukegan area nor those familiar with the particular variation of the Pace method performed on the patient. Although he testified that there was a national standard of care for the Pace method, he also stated that the Pace procedure was performed differently by different surgeons.

The trial court barred the patient's expert from testifying, finding that he lacked sufficient qualifications. The rule in Illinois required that the expert witness either demonstrate familiarity with the methods, procedures, and treatments ordinarily used by other physicians, either in the defendant's community or a similar locality, or establish that there was a national standard of care for the procedure in question. In this case, the expert failed to familiarize himself with the standard of care in Waukegan, Illinois, while the patient failed to establish that Toledo, Ohio, was a locality similar to Waukegan. Perhaps even more importantly, the patient's expert testified that the Pace procedure varied from location to location and that there was no consensus among surgeons as to the best way to perform it. Lacking familiarity with the standard of care in Waukegan or similar communities and in the absence of an articulated national standard of care, the expert witness was deemed not qualified to testify.

While the courts usually determine whether an expert witness is qualified to testify, it is the responsibility of the jury to evaluate an expert's testimony. In that sense, the jurors become the sole judges of the credibility of an expert witness, focusing on such things as his or her demeanor, memory, manner of testifying, and apparent bias, as well as the reasonableness of the expert's testimony when evaluated in relation to other evidence presented in the case. Weighing the usually contradictory opinions offered by the expert witnesses who testify for the two sides in a malpractice trial, the jurors must determine which are the more credible and persuasive, and this determination will have a significant bearing on their verdict.

Malpractice trials that involve the doctrine of *res ipsa loquitur* (literally translated, "the thing speaks for itself") may not require expert witnesses, however. When the doctrine is applied in a medical malpractice case, the court will permit the jury to draw an inference of negligence from circumstantial evidence. In such cases, the patient must prove (1) that the injury is of the kind that ordinarily does not occur in the absence of negligence, (2) that the injury was caused by an agency or instrumentality within the exclusive control of the defendant, and (3) that the injury was not due to any voluntary act or neglect on the part of the patient.

If the patient meets the burden of demonstrating those three things, the burden shifts to the defendant to prove that the event may occur even in the absence of negligence or that there are other reasonable causes for the event. In such a situation, expert testimony is not required to prove a violation of the standard of care.

Typically, the *res ipsa loquitur* doctrine is applied in cases such as those in which a sponge or other foreign object has been left inside a patient's body, when the patient has suffered severe X-ray burns, or in other similar situations. In applying the doctrine, the courts are essentially taking the position that the alleged negligence is so obviously or grossly apparent that a lay juror would have no difficulty in evaluating it, even in the absence of expert testimony.

The case of *Schaffner v. Cumberland County Hospital System, Inc.*, 336 S.E.2d 116 (N.C. App. 1985), offers an excellent example of how the court applied the *res ipsa loquitur* doctrine, thereby eliminating the plaintiff's obligation to introduce expert testimony to establish a violation of the standard of care.

In *Schaffner*, a surgeon scheduled surgical operation to remove the adenoids and insert drainage tubes in the ears of a child who experienced persistent ear infections. Following the surgical operation, the patient's mother and grandmother observed a burn on the patient's right hand that had not previously been there. To treat the burn, the patient was hospitalized for a skin graft. Following this procedure, a scar remained.

The patient filed suit against the surgeon and the hospital. The trial court granted summary judgment in favor of the defendants on the grounds that no expert evidence had been presented at trial to allow the jury to conclude that the defendants had been negligent. Appealing that decision, the patient argued that no expert evidence was necessary because the *res ipsa loquitur* doctrine would apply to the case. The court agreed. It observed that, although the patient had produced no expert testimony as to the cause of her injury, the surgeon's deposition had suggested that a malfunctioning hyfrecator used during the surgical operation could have been a possible cause for the burn. "[W]hen, as here, the facts can be evaluated based on common experience and knowledge, expert testimony is not required," the court stated, further holding that while any patient receiving medical treatment faces certain inherent risks, it is reasonable for a jury to conclude that being burned is not among them. Moreover, because the patient's burn would not ordinarily have occurred unless someone in control of the instrumentality that caused the injury was negligent, the court concluded that summary judgment in favor of the physicians was improper.

Causation

The legal connection between a surgeon's negligent act or omission and the injury that results therefrom is referred to as proximate causation. Proximate cause is usually defined as any cause that, in natural or probable sequence, results in an injury. The link between cause and result must be reasonably certain and cannot simply be speculative. Unless the causal linkage between injuries sustained by a patient and negligent acts or omissions is reasonably clear, the patient cannot recover damages in a medical malpractice lawsuit.

In *Guzman v. Faraldo*, 373 So.2d 66 (Fla. App. 1979), the patient's inability to demonstrate proximate causation between the injury and the surgeon's allegedly negligent conduct resulted in a directed verdict in favor of the surgeon.

The suit in *Guzman* was brought by a patient who had undergone open heart operation. Several days after the surgical operation, the patient's head was angled to one side and she could not control her neck muscles. An examination revealed damage to the patient's eleventh cranial nerve. The patient and her husband filed suit alleging that the nerve damage had occurred during surgical operation because of improper positioning of the patient's body while she was under general anesthetic.

The patient introduced expert testimony that improper positioning could cause injury of the nature she had sustained. The patient's evidence further showed that the surgeon had not seen the positioning of the patient's head during the operation and that no other available witness was able to testify as to the intubation of the patient or her positioning. Expert testimony introduced by the defendant emphasized that no such injury during this type of surgical operation had ever been discussed in the medical literature and that damage to the eleventh cranial nerve could occur in a variety of ways, including as a result of degenerative disease, inflammation of the nerve, pressure from tumors, and so on. The patient herself testified that she initially had thought the nerve damage was the result of a car accident.

At the close of the patient's case, the trial judge ordered a directed verdict in favor of both the surgeon and the hospital. On appeal, the reviewing court evaluated the evidence and concluded that "[u]nder the circumstances, where the evidence fails to show a causal connection between the injury complained of and the breach of the standard of reasonable care, the trial court properly directed a verdict for the defendants." While the patient in this case failed to prove, by the greater weight of evidence, that the injuries sustained were the natural and probable consequence of allegedly negligent conduct, expert medical testimony at trial can have the opposite effect.

This opposite effect was shown in *Hauser v. Bhatnager*, 537 A.2d 599 (Me. 1988).

The defendant in *Hauser*, a plastic surgeon, had seen the patient about correcting the positioning of her right eyebrow, which was slightly lower than the left. The surgeon suggested surgical operation to lift the right eyebrow, performing it a few days later in his office under local anesthetic. Five days after the procedure, the patient was examined by the surgeon, who found that the wound was healing well.

Another follow-up appointment was scheduled for the patient, but she failed to keep it, traveling instead to California. While in California, the patient experienced itching and numbness of the forehead and consulted a general surgeon, who identified the condition as paresthesia. After removing the stitches in the patient's forehead, the general surgeon found that the wound was healing properly, with an acceptable fine line scar. The general surgeon saw the patient again several months later. This time he found that the scar was a quarter inch wide, depressed, and brown in color.

The patient filed suit against the plastic surgeon based on several legal theories, including malpractice, and a jury awarded her $10,000. The surgeon appealed that decision, arguing that the patient's negligence claim should have been rejected because of insufficient evidence of causation. The court noted the applicable legal standard, stating, "The verdict must be sustained if any credible evidence, and all justifiable inferences drawn from such evidence, viewed in the light most favorable to the plaintiff, support the verdict." The court observed that the patient's expert had testified that her paresthesia was caused by the defendant's failure to protect her supraorbital nerve during the surgical operation and that, further, the patient's scarring was caused by the defendant's failure to properly close her incision.

Given this credible expert evidence, the court concluded that the jury verdict had to be upheld. The court also rejected the defendant's argument that the jury was required to find that the patient had caused the injury herself to some degree by failing to keep her second follow-up appointment with him. From the evidence presented, the court held, "[t]he jury was free to conclude that the plaintiff's failure to keep the appointment did not cause or contribute to the . . . scarring or nerve damage . . . ."

Damages

Awarding monetary damages is the way in which a remedy is provided to individuals who sustain injury as the proximate result of negligent conduct by a physician. Typically, damages are intended to compensate for loss or injury sustained by the patient. In cases involving gross negligence, an injured party may also be entitled to an award of punitive damages, depending on the state in which the action is brought.

Compensatory Damages

Monetary damages awarded to compensate a wrongfully injured person are referred to as compensatory damages. A medical malpractice plaintiff may recover such damages for a variety of losses, including those related to the reasonable expense of medical care and treatment necessitated by the injury; the value of earnings, salaries, and profits lost and reasonably certain to be lost in the future as a result of it; aggravation of a pre-existing ailment; and the patient's pain and suffering.

Another recognized basis for the award of compensatory damages in medical malpractice litigation is loss of consortium. Such awards typically reflect losses sustained by one spouse as the result of injury to the other. A jury may award compensatory damages for loss of consortium on the basis of the reasonable value of the companionship, society, and conjugal relationship of which a spouse has been deprived and is reasonably certain to be deprived in the future. Damages also may be awarded on the basis of loss of consortium between parents and children when, for example, parents are deprived of the society of a child who dies as the result of medical malpractice.

Damages also may be awarded to compensate a surviving spouse or the next of kin for pecuniary injuries suffered. Among the factors that may be considered by a jury in awarding such damages are the customary contributions of the decedent in the past; his or her former and likely future earnings; and the value of any instruction, training, and supervision of education that the decedent might reasonably have been expected to provide to the family had death not occurred. A surviving spouse also might recover such expenditures as hospital, medical, and funeral costs incurred in connection with the decedent's death.

In *Reager v. Anderson*, 371 S.E.2d 619 (W.Va. 1988), the court's discussion of the basis for the jury's damage award is instructive.

Reager involved a claim by a 13-year-old boy and his father against a general surgeon and an orthopaedic surgeon for negligence that resulted in the amputation of the boy's left leg. The orthopaedic surgeon allegedly had been negligent in failing to see the boy in a timely fashion, failing to diagnose an injury to his popliteal artery, and failing to debride dead tissue in his leg upon discovery.

While the general surgeon agreed to settle the case after all the evidence had been presented at trial, the orthopaedic surgeon did not. Following a jury verdict of approximately $1.27 million in favor of the patient and his father, the orthopaedic surgeon appealed to the West Virginia Supreme Court. Among various arguments, he asserted that evidence regarding projected costs related to a novel prosthetic device and of the boy's loss of future earnings was speculative and therefore should not have been considered by the jury.

At trial, the patient's expert witness had testified that the annual maintenance cost of a novel prosthetic device needed by the boy, when reduced to present value, was

II / Substantive Tort Law

$260,000. This estimate was based on costs related to conventional prosthetic devices on the grounds that, while the plaintiff's device was novel, it incorporated many of the same components of more conventional devices. The jury also heard estimates of the patient's lost future earnings from his economic expert and a vocational rehabilitation expert, who testified, without dispute, that these lost future earnings would range from $192,230 to $1,155,000, based on five possible vocational scenarios in which the potential earnings of a person with two legs was compared with those of a person with only one leg.

The appellate court rejected the defendant orthopaedic surgeon's argument that this evidence was too speculative, finding it adequate to support the jury's damage award. The court further stated that, even if those particular damage claims were not considered, the evidence in the record would support an award of damages in the same amount for the patient's pain and suffering alone.

A jury's determination of the amount of damages to award a patient must reasonably be based on evidence presented during the course of a trial, and courts will place great weight on the jury's decision. Unless a damage award was clearly based on sympathy or prejudice, courts rarely overturn or alter the amount of damages awarded by juries.

As *Merrill v. Albany Medical Center Hospital*, 512 N.Y.S. 2d 519 (App. Div. 1987), demonstrates, however, a court may reduce a jury verdict that it finds to be excessive and the apparent product of sympathy or prejudice.

Merrill involved a 22-month-old child, diagnosed as having a possible malignant tumor on her right lung, who experienced cardiac arrest during surgical operation to remove the tumor. Although the surgeon was able to restore the patient's heart beat by manual massage, she remained comatose for two months and was later determined to have suffered severe brain damage as a result of oxygen deprivation during the incident.

Suit was filed against the surgeon, various anesthesiologists involved with the surgical operation, and the hospital. At the end of a six-week-long trial, but prior to closing arguments, a $2 million settlement was agreed to by all of the parties except the surgeon. The case then was submitted to the jury for a decision related to the surgeon's liability, without disclosure to them of the settlement amount.

The jury apportioned percentages of liability among the various defendants, assessing the surgeon's liability at three percent. The jury set the patient's total damages at almost $12.4 million and her mother's damages at $261,000. After reducing these amounts to $10.4 million and $177,000, respectively, based on evidentiary considerations, the trial court apportioned three percent of each amount to the surgeon.

The surgeon appealed, arguing that the jury's damage verdict was excessive, even as reduced by the trial judge. The appellate court reviewed the uncontested testimony regarding the patient's condition as a result of her injuries, noting that she was blind, could neither talk nor ambulate on her own, was spastic, and had cerebral palsy and, therefore, would need extensive assistance for the rest of her life. This evidence, the court noted, "would engender sympathy in abundance even from the most calloused sort." The jury was in an understandably difficult position "and may well have been overcome with sympathy," the court concluded, ordering a new trial on the issue of damages unless the patient agreed to reduce the total damage award to $6.1 million.

Punitive Damages

In addition to compensatory damages, some states also permit punitive damages to be awarded when the evidence in a medical malpractice trial establishes that a surgeon has acted willfully or with negligence so gross as to indicate a wanton disregard for the patient's rights.

The objective of punitive damages is to punish a wrongdoer, thereby presumably deterring others from committing similar wrongs. Punitive damages often are awarded in product liability cases in which serious harm has been caused as a result of defects in the design, manufacture, testing, or marketing of a product. Juries have also awarded punitive damages in cases in which a manufacturer knew, or reasonably should have known, of dangers associated with use of a product, but failed to adequately warn consumers about the product's dangers or defects.

While awards of punitive damages are not uncommon in product liability litigation, awarding them in medical malpractice cases has never been favored by the law. The courts are therefore inclined to carefully evaluate the facts of any case in which punitive damages are at issue.

The court in *Tonelli v. Khanna*, 569 A.2d 282 (N.J. Super. 1990), illustrates this point.

The patient in *Tonelli* was referred to a radiologist for a sonogram because of pain and lumps in her left breast. The radiologist reported a "well-circumscribed, well-outlined" area in the patient's breast that was "probably cystic in origin." Believing the condition to be lobular hyperplasia, he recommended a biopsy. Based on this information, the patient's family physician suggested that she see a surgeon. The patient's prior medical reports were read over the telephone to the surgeon, who subsequently examined the patient. Feeling a lump in her breast, he recommended that it promptly be surgically removed.

The evidence presented at trial as to whether the surgeon discussed the consequences of the surgical operation with the patient was conflicting, although the surgeon maintained that there had been such a discussion, and the patient had signed a consent form. When the surgical operation was performed, the tissue removed showed fibrocystic breast disease. While later visiting friends in Florida, the patient experienced a postoperative infection and was given antibiotics. After returning home, she began to see another physician, who treated her condition with hormones, vitamins, and dietary changes.

The patient sued the surgeon, claiming, in part, that his performance of the unnecessary surgical operation without her informed consent was an intentional wrong, entitling her to punitive damages. Following a jury verdict of $10,000 for the patient, she appealed, arguing that, based on the evidence she had presented, the jury could have concluded that the defendant had performed the unnecessary operation for his own financial gain and that punitive damages were thus called for. However, a review of the evidence convinced the appellate court that the trial judge had properly rejected the patient's claim of an intentional wrong as wholly unsupported by the evidence. "To warrant a punitive damages award, defendant's conduct must have been an intentional wrong . . . or accompanied by wanton and willful disregard of the rights of others," the court concluded.

Contract Liability

While most medical malpractice actions in the United States are based on the legal principles of tort law or negligence, some have been based on contract principles. For that reason, physicians should at least be aware of the circumstances under which such actions may arise.

As a general rule, two types of contracts are recognized under the law: express contracts and implied contracts. An express contract is entered into when the parties to it reach a specific agreement as a result of an exchange of written or spoken words. The terms and conditions of express contracts are usually set forth with specificity, clearly delineating the rights and responsibilities of the parties. In contrast, the obligations of the parties in implied contracts are not specifically delineated, but, rather, are imposed as a matter of law, usually on the basis of the particular relationship between the parties. For example, when a surgeon agrees to provide treatment to a patient, the law imposes an implicit obligation on the surgeon to use reasonable skill and care in providing that treatment.

Lawsuits against a surgeon based on a breach of an implied contract are rare, but litigation against physicians and surgeons involving express contracts is not unknown. Most medical malpractice lawsuits based on contract theory allege the breach of an express promise by a physician or surgeon, such as a promise to cure a particular illness or achieve a particular outcome. As a general rule, however, the courts have not been inclined to recognize that express promises exist in the physician-patient relationship. To the contrary, most courts understand that a physician's statements to a patient are most likely to be expressions of opinion that are intended to afford therapeutic reassurance. A surgeon may, however, inadvertently make an express promise to a patient that either constitutes more than therapeutic reassurance or guarantees the accomplishment of a specific result or results. When that occurs, the courts may permit a patient to sue on the basis of breach of a contractual promise or guarantee, even in situations in which the surgeon has utilized proper skill and care in providing treatment.

In *Scarzella v. Saxon*, 436 A.2d 358 (D.C. App. 1981), for example, the patient was diagnosed as having diverticulum of the urethra.

The defendant in *Scarzella*, a urologist, recommended surgical operation to remove the diverticulum. The patient alleged that the urologist had assured her and her husband in a discussion prior to the surgical operation that the procedure would be simple and without complications, that it would require only a very short hospital stay, and that it would interfere only temporarily with the patient's work and the couple's sexual relations. These assurances were allegedly reiterated at a subsequent meeting, after which the patient consented to the surgical operation. Complications from the operation developed, necessitating two additional operations and leaving the patient with chronic problems. As a result, the patient and her husband filed suit against the urologist based on a breach of express warranty theory.

The appellate court upheld a judgment of $75,000 for the patient based upon the trial court's instruction to the jury that, to find a breach of warranty, "the language or statement used or alleged to have been used by the surgeon must be clearly and unmistakably a positive assurance . . . to produce or to avoid a particular result . . . ." While the court acknowledged that a physician does not typically warrant a specific result or cure, it observed that, in some circumstances, a physician's representations may create such an obligation. In this case, the appellate court found that the trial court's instructions had adequately protected the defendant from a frivolous warranty claim, while properly allowing for such a claim in situations where a warranty actually had been made.

It should be emphasized that, despite this example, a patient who brings suit against a surgeon based on the breach of contract theory bears the arduous legal burden of alleging and proving that a specific guarantee or express promise has been made, as well as proving that the patient relied on that promise in deciding to undergo the treatment. Because of the difficulty of proving that those things have occurred, such cases typically result in a ruling or judgment in favor of the surgeon.

Thus, more typical than *Scarzella* is *Van Zee v. Witzke*, 445 N.W.2d 34 (S.D. 1989), in which the appellate court upheld a judgment in favor of a reconstructive and plastic surgeon.

In *Van Zee*, the patient claimed that a surgeon had expressly agreed to cure a deformity of her finger that had occurred as a result of a childhood accident, a deformity that would cause her finger to "lock" when she typed, thereby impeding her work as a court reporter. The patient consulted the surgeon, who found metallic sutures in the flexor tender and a hyperextension of the first joint of the finger. Three months later, after a second examination, surgical operation was performed. Subsequently, an infection occurred, which the surgeon treated. The surgeon also referred the patient to a physical therapist who, during one session, broke the patient's finger, which required additional treatment by the surgeon.

After healing, the patient's finger remained stiff, had a slight deformity of the distal tip, and was largely useless to her. She therefore sued the surgeon, basing her suit on several theories of law, including breach of an express contract.

On appeal, the South Dakota Supreme Court upheld the trial court's judgment in favor of the surgeon on the contract theory, observing that the defendant's office notes showed that he had thoroughly discussed the risks and problems of the surgical operation with the patient. The court further noted that the patient had told her mother prior to the surgical operation that no physician would guarantee results. The court found that the defendant's alleged statement that the patient's finger would be no worse following surgical operation than it had been prior to surgical operation was simply insufficient to constitute an express contract to heal her finger.

Despite the fact that the courts are generally inclined to rule against patients who sue surgeons on the basis of contract theory, the fact that such actions may be brought argues strongly for physicians to carefully avoid making express promises that may be viewed as representing more than therapeutic reassurance or entering into written or verbal agreements guaranteeing the accomplishment of a specific result.

Liability for the Acts of Others

When one individual is authorized to act for or on behalf of another, a so-called *agency relationship* is established under the law. The parties to such a relationship may be referred to as the *principal and agent* or as the *master and servant*.

Under principles of agency law, the principal is legally responsible for the negligent conduct of an agent. This accountability, which is referred to as *vicarious liability*, constitutes the mechanism by which the law has endeavored to maximize the likelihood that a person who is harmed as a result of the conduct of another person will be fully compensated. The law allows for imposition of this liability on the basis of the "deep pocket" theory, under which the principal in an agency relationship is viewed as being more capable of absorbing the costs of liability and is thus held responsible for the negligent acts or omissions of an agent. The doctrine of vicarious liability most commonly applies to the employer-employee relationship, making employers legally responsible for the negligent conduct of their employees.

Respondeat Superior

The application of vicarious liability principles also is referred to by the Latin phrase, *respondeat superior*, "let the master respond." This legal doctrine holds employers responsible for the negligent conduct of employees that occurs during the course of their employment. Under this doctrine, the employer may be held liable whether or not the employer approved the employee's action or, for that matter, even knew about or observed the negligent conduct. A surgeon thus may be held vicariously liable for the negligent conduct of an employee nurse, receptionist, or office worker. Similarly, a medical or service corporation may be liable for the negligent conduct of its employees.

Most cases discussing the doctrine of vicarious liability focus on liability of hospitals and other health care institutions that arises out of the negligence of their employees, holding such institutions liable when personnel, such as staff nurses, laboratory personnel, and X-ray technicians negligently cause injury to a patient.

The case of *Joyce v. National Medical Registry, Inc.*, 524 N.E.2d 243 (Ill. App. 1988), demonstrates how this doctrine is applied.

Joyce focused on the question of which one of several defendants might have been vicariously liable for the negligence of a nurse-anesthetist who, it was alleged, caused an infant to go into cardiac arrest during surgical operation and eventually die as a result of an error in the administration of anesthesia. The suit, filed by the infant's parents, sought damages for the child's wrongful death from an array of defendants, including the surgeon, the anesthesiologist, the nurse-anesthetist, the hospital, and an employment agency that had provided the nurse-anesthetist to the hospital on temporary assignment. The parents claimed that the nurse was an employee of this employment agency, which thus was liable for her actions. When the agency successfully moved for a dismissal of the action against it, the parents appealed the decision.

The appellate court outlined factors to consider in determining whether an employment relationship existed, among them: "(1) the right to control the manner of performance of the work; (2) whether compensation was by time or job; (3) the right to discharge; (4) the nature and duration of the occupation; (5) who furnishes the equipment used and support personnel; and (6) the right to control the time, place, and scope of work." Taking these factors into account, the court concluded that the nurse was not the employee of the agency. While the agency paid her salary, it found that the facts showed that others, including the hospital to which she was assigned, controlled her work, supplied equipment for her use, and had the right to discharge her. Accordingly, the court determined that, for purposes of vicarious liability, the nurse was not an employee of the agency.

Even in situations where an employment relationship is found to exist, not all wrongful conduct of an employee will result in vicarious liability for an employer, unless the conduct occurred within the scope of the employment relationship. Therefore, if the employee had committed an intentionally wrongful act that was not within the scope of his or her employment, vicarious liability principles usually would not apply.

For example, in *Noto v. St. Vincent's Hospital & Medical Center*, 537 N.Y.S.2d 446 (Sup. Ct. 1988), a hospital was not found to be vicariously liable for an employee's wrongful conduct.

The patient in *Noto* had sought care at the hospital for depression, drug and alcohol abuse, and "seductive behavior." The patient claimed that she and a psychiatrist in the hospital's graduate residency program who provided her care had developed a "close relationship," which continued after the psychiatrist rotated off her case. Following the patient's discharge, she and the psychiatrist entered into a sexual relationship, which also allegedly involved the use of drugs and alcohol. After terminating the relationship, the patient filed suit against the psychiatrist and the hospital, basing her claim against the hospital on its status as the psychiatrist's employer under the *respondeat superior* doctrine.

The court noted that the employer's liability under the doctrine depends upon whether "the tortious conduct of the employee [was] in furtherance of the employer's business and within the scope of the employer's authority" and concluded that the hospital was not liable for the psychiatrist's acts. In the court's view, the psychiatrist's conduct was clearly not in furtherance of the hospital's business, but, rather, of his own personal affairs. Further, the court said, the psychiatrist's actions exceeded his authority and certainly were not a "natural incident of his employment or duties."

The Borrowed Servant and Captain of the Ship Doctrines

The *borrowed servant* doctrine, in which the employee or servant of one master is temporarily borrowed by another who exercises specific control over that person to accomplish a particular purpose, represents another application of vicarious liability principles.

When a third party temporarily "borrows" the "servant" of another "master" and exercises supervision and control over the servant's conduct, vicarious liability principles may apply to the temporary master. For example, when a surgeon directly controls the conduct of a hospital employee as an aspect of a particular course of treatment, the employee becomes a borrowed servant of the surgeon. Should negligent conduct of the borrowed servant result in injury to a patient, the surgeon may be vicariously liable for the injury.

The most common application of this doctrine in medical malpractice litigation arises when patient injury is caused by negligence that occurs in a hospital operating room. Ruling in this context, the courts traditionally have held the chief surgeon vicariously liable for negligence of members of the surgical team whose conduct the surgeon has the right to control. Drawing an analogy, some courts have referred to the chief surgeon in the operating room as the *"captain of the ship,"* a phrase by which the doctrine also may be known. Indeed, extending the captain of the ship analogy, some courts have expanded the borrowed servant doctrine to hold the chief surgeon responsible for negligence of other personnel in the operating room, whether or not the surgeon has the right to exercise control over their actions.

More recently, however, courts have come to recognize that some members of the operating room team perform highly specialized and independent functions that may not come under the direct control and supervision of the surgeon. Rather than automatically imposing the borrowed servant doctrine, the courts will, instead, evaluate the question of whether or not the chief surgeon had direct control and supervision over a hospital employee whose conduct was negligent. In making that determination, they will focus on the specific responsibilities of the hospital employee relative to the applicable clinical facts and circumstances, also taking into account applicable custom and practice.

In the case of *Baird v. Sickler*, 433 N.E.2d 593 (Ohio 1982), an Ohio court, making that determination, held that the evidence was clear that the surgeon defendant had in fact assumed direct control of the conduct of a hospital employee.

The surgeon in *Baird* had performed a laminectomy to treat Klippel-Feil syndrome in a patient who also suffered from spondylosis. Rendered a C-6 paraplegic during the operation, the patient sued the surgeon. Evidence was introduced at trial to suggest that the patient's paralysis had resulted either from faulty positioning and intubation or aggravation of a minor intubation injury through sustained hypotension during the laminectomy.

Anesthesia for the surgical operation had been provided by a nurse-anesthetist employed by an agency under contract with the hospital. The surgeon, who had helped the nurse-anesthetist position the patient's head and torso for intubation, testified that he had instructed the anesthetist regarding the preferred intubation technique and position, watched the intubation, and would have halted the procedure had he observed any misfeasance. He had not, however, performed the actual insertion of the endotracheal tube.

The trial court directed a verdict in favor of the surgeon, finding that no reasonable juror could conclude that the surgeon was responsible for the nurse-anesthetist's negligence. The appeals court noted, however, that a master-servant relationship exists when a party possesses and exercises a right to control another's actions, and those actions are in furtherance of the master's objectives. Further, the court held, if a master lends his servant to another, the servant is deemed to be the servant of the borrower, even though the servant continues to be paid by his master. Under this analogy, the court held that, although an operating physician is not responsible for overseeing each detail that occurs in the highly technical environment of an operating room, a surgeon who controls or has the right to control a procedure may be liable for the negligence of a nonemployee who performs the procedure. The patient therefore prevailed on appeal.

II / Substantive Tort Law

Despite this particular ruling, the courts are increasingly reluctant to utilize the captain of the ship analogy and impose liability on a surgeon unless there is convincing evidence that a hospital employee was functioning under the surgeon's direct control and supervision. Arthur Southwick, a noted commentator on hospital law, has observed that, when medical care is provided by a sophisticated and highly specialized team of professionals working in the institutional setting, it is difficult to determine who is exercising direct control over whom at any given point in time. Thus, he views as reasonable the tendency of the courts to hold hospitals rather than private physicians liable for the conduct of hospital employees.

That trend is reflected in *Franklin v. Gupta*, 567 A.2d (Md. App. 1990), in which the court demonstrated its unwillingness to apply the captain of the ship doctrine and find a surgeon vicariously liable for the negligence of hospital employees without evidence that the surgeon had in fact exercised control over the conduct of those employees.

In *Franklin*, suit was brought by a patient who had undergone surgical operation for carpal tunnel syndrome. The patient, who was a "high-risk patient for anesthesia," developed complications during the surgical operation, becoming cyanotic, bradycardic, and asystolic, allegedly as a result of the negligence of the anesthesiologist and the nurse-anesthetist. Although the patient's heartbeat was restored and he was revived, the surgical operation had to be canceled. The patient thereafter filed an action against the anesthesiologist, the nurse-anesthetists, the hospital, and the surgeon. Because there was no evidence that the surgeon had in any way supervised or controlled the anesthesiologist or the nurse-anesthetist during the surgical operation, the trial court declined to instruct the jury on the captain of the ship doctrine, and the jury rendered a verdict in favor of the surgeon. The patient appealed, arguing that the trial judge had failed to properly instruct the jury on the law it was to apply to the surgeon's possible liability. The appellate court upheld the trial court's decision not to apply the doctrine. Observing the trend to reject the captain of the ship doctrine as an inappropriate expansion of the traditional borrowed servant rule, the court absolved the surgeon of legal responsibility for the acts of hospital employees, unless it could be shown that the surgeon had in fact exercised control over them during surgical operation.

Defenses

The frequency and severity of medical malpractice litigation in the United States is a matter of record. Nonetheless, a substantial number of claims are successfully concluded, without payment of a settlement or damage award, thanks, in large part, to the availability of a number of substantive, procedural, and statutory defenses.

Adherence to the Standard of Care

Introduction of evidence establishing that the surgeon complied with the applicable standard of care is the most important defense in a medical malpractice lawsuit. It should be emphasized that, in applying this defense, it is not necessary to measure the surgeon's conduct against the *highest* degree of skill possible. Indeed, it is sufficient to demonstrate only that the surgeon possessed and applied the knowledge, skill, and care *ordinarily* used by reasonably well-qualified surgeons practicing in similar cases and circumstances.

Nor is a surgeon obligated to be a guarantor of satisfactory results, and the fact that a surgical procedure or course of treatment is unsuccessful does not in itself constitute evidence of negligence. Unless the surgeon's conduct deviated from the standard of care, an honest mistake will not result in liability. Moreover, when alternate acceptable treatment methodologies are available, selection by a surgeon of one method over another is not alone likely to form a basis for liability.

The court underscored these considerations in *MacGuineas v. United States*, 738 F. Supp. 566 (D.D.C. 1990).

Brought after a patient had died from shock due to intraoperative hemorrhage resulting from laceration of her left innominate vein by a subclavian vein catheter, *MacGuineas* alleged negligence on the part of the surgeon. The surgical procedure had been performed to place a Port-A-Cath system in the patient to assist in treatment of her Hodgkin's disease.

At the time of the surgical operation, the patient's cancer had progressed to stage III, and she had recently been treated with both chemotherapy and radiation therapy, which necessitated repeated invasive procedures. After she volunteered to participate in a National Cancer Institute study, comparing the site infection rates of two commonly used catheter systems, the risks of the operation were explained to the patient, and she agreed to the procedure.

Insertion of the catheter was attempted on the left side. During the operation, difficulties were encountered in attempting to pass the catheter into the vein. After a second attempt to place the catheter, the patient's blood pressure dropped precipitously, and emergency procedures were initiated. A 5-mm tear in the patient's left innominate vein was repaired, but the patient went into a coma and died two days later.

In filing suit, the patient's estate argued that the surgical operation had been done on the wrong side of the patient's body, that the surgeons had failed to use radiopaque confirmation of the placement of the guide wire for the catheter, that the wrong size dilator had been used, that excessive force had been employed in trying to insert the catheter, and that the procedure should have been discontinued when resistance to insertion of the catheter was encountered. Eight physicians testified at the trial. Except for one who testified that the surgeons should have moved to her right side when difficulties in inserting the catheter on the left were encountered, all agreed that the defendants had met the proper standard of care.

Rendering a judgment for the defendants, the court noted that a physician is not required to use "the highest degree of care known to the profession," but, rather, "that reasonable degree of care and skill which physicians and surgeons ordinarily exercise in the treatment of their patients." While "it was obvious to everyone that something went wrong" during the surgical operation, the court stated, it was equally "clear that the existence of the laceration does not automatically mean that the standard of care was violated." Given the inexact nature of medicine, and keeping in mind the severity of the patient's medical problems and the complexity of the procedure, the court concluded that the surgeons had exercised a reasonable degree of skill and care and were not liable for the unfortunate outcome.

As the court acknowledged in *MacGuineas*, medicine is not an exact science. Differences of professional opinion do exist, and an expert's testimony that he or she might have performed a surgical procedure differently is not adequate to prove negligence. Instead, evidence must establish, more probably than not, that a surgeon's conduct violated the applicable standard of care and that the conduct proximately caused injury to the patient. Even when such evidence is introduced by a patient, a surgeon can meaningfully defend against it by providing credible expert evidence demonstrating that the surgeon's conduct did not violate the applicable standard of care.

Statutes of Limitation

Statutes of limitation are intended to establish a particular time frame within which medical malpractice litigation must be initiated. Intended to foster timely prosecution of litigation, these statutes are designed to ensure that a defendant's ability to muster an adequate defense is not compromised because witnesses or other evidence are no longer available.

Although the specific statutory period within which medical malpractice litigation must be commenced varies from state to state, the period in most states is approximately two years following the date on which a claimant knew, or through the use of reasonable diligence should have known, about the injury or death for which damages are sought. In some states, the statute of limitations may specify an absolute date beyond which litigation may not be commenced. Should a patient file a lawsuit after the applicable statutory period has concluded, the surgeon may interpose the procedural defense of the statute of limitations. Such a defense is characterized as *procedural*, because it essentially blocks the patient from prosecuting a claim, without regard for the merits of the claim.

As historically applied by the courts, the statutory limitations period begins on the date of the last act of negligence that gave rise to the patient's claim. Thus, it was possible that the statutory period could lapse before a patient even learned of a negligently caused injury, as, for example, could occur in the event that a foreign object that was difficult to detect had been left in the patient's body during surgical operation. In an effort to minimize the impact of strict application of statutes of limitations, the courts have adopted a rule known as the *discovery rule*.

In accordance with the discovery rule, the period of limitation begins when a patient knows, or reasonably should know, of an injury and also is aware, or reasonably should be aware, that the injury was wrongfully caused.

In *Juravle v. Ozdagler*, 385 N.W.2d 627 (Mich. App. 1985), for example, the court made it clear that a statutory limitations period may not commence until the patient is reasonably aware of the existence of a medical problem or injury, as well as the possibility that the surgeon was negligent.

The patient in *Juravle* had sought an internist's treatment for chronic abdominal pain. The internist hospitalized the patient with a diagnosis of cholecystitis, then referred him to a surgeon, who performed an exploratory laparotomy on April 17, 1978, intending to also perform a cholecystectomy. However, unable to locate the patient's gallbladder, the surgeon theorized that it must already have been removed. The surgeon provided follow-up care until June 2, 1978.

The patient continued to experience abdominal pain and consulted attorneys in March 1980. In April 1980, he was hospitalized by another surgeon, informed that he did, indeed, have a gallbladder, and advised that the organ should be removed. On May 28, 1980, the patient retrieved his medical records from the defendant-surgeon's office; however, the parties disputed whether the surgeon conducted an examination at that time. The patient's gallbladder was removed on September 11, 1980.

On April 22, 1981, the patient filed suit against the internist and the surgeon. Under the law of the state in which the suit was filed, a malpractice claim had to be filed within two years after the defendant's last treatment, or within six months after discovery of the claim. Because the relevant medical treatment had been rendered more than two years prior to the suit's filing, the claims against the internist and the surgeon were dismissed.

On appeal, the court found that the statute of limitations relevant to the claim against the surgeon had begun to run on June 2, 1978, when follow-up care for the laparotomy ceased. The patient contended that he was still within the limitation period because he had filed suit within six months of discovery of the malpractice claim. The court outlined a two-part test to determine the date of discovery for purposes of the statute. According to the court, the limitations period would begin (1) when the act or omission of the physician became known to the patient, and (2) when the patient "has reason to believe that the medical treatment either was improper or was performed in an improper manner."

The court held that the first test was satisfied on April 26, 1980, when the patient was informed that he had a gallbladder. It further held that the second test was satisfied soon thereafter when he consulted with an attorney who advised him to file suit after his cholecystectomy.

Because the suit had not been filed until April 22, 1981, almost one year after discovery, it was dismissed.

As already noted, some states have established a maximum period within which a malpractice lawsuit must be filed, regardless of the applicability of the discovery rule. For example, a statute may establish a two-year limitations period and a maximum four-year period of repose. In such a situation, a patient would be able to bring a lawsuit at any time up to two years following the date when he or she knew, or reasonably should have known, of an injury and also knew, or reasonably should have known, that it was caused by negligence.

If, however, more than four years had elapsed since the negligent conduct occurred, the patient would be precluded from commencing litigation because of the maximum four-year period of repose. Thus, when a patient does not discover medical malpractice until one year after the negligent act in question, the patient has two years from the discovery date within which to file the litigation—that is, three years from the date of the last negligent conduct. If, however, a patient discovered the medical malpractice three and a half years following the date of negligent conduct, the patient would have to initiate litigation within six months of the discovery date in order to meet the four-year filing requirement. A patient who did not discover a negligently caused injury until four and a half years after the negligent conduct would be forever barred from initiating litigation.

A Louisiana case, *Valentine v. Thomas*, 433 So.2d 289 (La. App. 1983), illustrates the operation of a statute of repose.

In *Valentine*, the patient was operated on in 1977 for traumatic acromioclavicular separation, the surgeon using two Kirschner's wires during the procedure. Several months after the surgical operation, in early 1978, the surgeon saw the patient and removed two portions of the wire from his shoulder. In March 1981, the patient consulted another physician, who x-rayed him and found a small portion of wire still in his shoulder. The wire was surgically removed. In March 1982, the patient filed suit against the surgeon who had performed the 1977 operation.

Louisiana law provided a one-year statute of limitations for malpractice claims against physicians, with a three-year statute of repose. Because the patient had not discovered the presence of the wire until more than three years after he had last been seen by the defendant surgeon, the trial court ruled he could not bring his claim. On appeal, the patient challenged the constitutionality of the repose statute as being in violation of the equal protection and due process clauses of the state's constitution. The appellate court rejected these arguments. The court noted the legislature's objective in enacting the statute—that is, "the alleviation of the insurance crisis by reducing medical malpractice claims, thereby reducing medical malpractice insurance rates, resulting in health care being more accessible to patients at reasonable costs"—and found that, while injuries may not be discoverable for many years, "three years is a reasonable length of time for acts of malpractice to be discovered and suits to be instituted therefor." Thus, it held, it is not inconsistent with public policy for state law to establish a maximum time frame within which medical malpractice litigation must be initiated.

Despite these considerations, most limitations statutes identify various disabilities on the part of a patient that prevent the limitations period from beginning to run. Among others, protection is afforded to minors, persons imprisoned on criminal charges, and those who are mentally disabled or incompetent. In the case of a minor, limitations statutes typically either provide an extended period within which a malpractice lawsuit must be initiated or delay the start of the limitations period until the minor reaches adulthood. Such statutory protection ensures that minors will not necessarily be deprived of their rights to pursue a malpractice claim simply because their parents failed to file a timely lawsuit on their behalf.

II / Substantive Tort Law

Similarly, the law is unwilling to hold a person who is mentally disabled or incompetent accountable for failing to initiate a malpractice lawsuit in accordance with the applicable statute of limitations. Ordinarily, the limitations period for a mentally disabled or incompetent person does not begin to run until the disability is removed. Similar protection is afforded in various states to persons imprisoned on criminal charges, thus precluding the limitations period from beginning until the disability or imprisonment is removed.

When surgical care is provided to individuals who are under a legal disability that blocks the statute of limitations from running, a surgeon must be cognizant of the extended period of liability. In fact, because medical malpractice litigation in such cases may be initiated many years after the last date of treatment, despite statutes of limitation, surgeons are well advised to retain medical records for as long a time as possible.

Patient Negligence

Although a surgeon may be held liable for injuries proximately caused by his or her negligent conduct or the negligent conduct of third parties on the basis of vicarious liability, a surgeon may not be liable for injuries that result when a patient fails to follow the surgeon's specific instructions or from the patient's delay in obtaining surgical treatment.

That fact is amply demonstrated in *Butler v. Berkeley*, 213 S.E.2d 571 (N.C. App. 1975).

In *Butler*, a plastic surgeon had installed a steel prosthetic device and silicone implants in a patient's face to correct a congenital abnormality. On the tenth postoperative day, the patient had removed the nasogastric feeding tube that had been placed to prevent contamination of his oral incision. Refusing to permit a nurse to reinsert the tube, the patient called the surgeon to explain that his refusal was based on "nerves" and nausea. Six weeks later, after his discharge from the hospital, the pin was removed from the patient's cheek, at which time an infection became apparent, which necessitated removal of a silicone disc and necrotic bone. The patient later filed suit, alleging negligent failure to observe sterile technique, failure to remove certain bone fragments in the surgical area, and negligent postoperative care.

The trial court granted judgment for the surgeon, and the judgment was affirmed on appeal. Because the evidence established that the oral ingestion of food against the surgeon's orders was a proximate cause of infection, the court held that the patient was "the sole author of his misfortune."

There are, of course, instances in which both the patient and the surgeon are negligent. Depending upon the law of the individual state, the extent of a patient's negligence in such cases will bear upon the question of the surgeon's liability, as well as on the amount of damages that may be recovered.

Under the traditional negligence doctrine, a jury's conclusion that a patient's negligence contributed in any way to an injury would preclude the patient from recovering damages against the surgeon. Referred to as *contributory negligence*, this bar to recovery was viewed as harsh and unfair by many state courts and legislatures. Accordingly, most, if not all, states have replaced the doctrine of contributory negligence with the doctrine of *comparative negligence*. Under this latter doctrine, a patient's negligence has an important bearing on the amount of damages that may be recovered, although it is only in situations in which the negligence is substantial that recovery may be totally barred.

Under the pure form of comparative negligence, a jury is required to determine whether a patient's injury is proximately caused by a combination of the negligence of the patient and the negligence of one or more of the defendants. If so, the jury is instructed to determine the damages to which the patient would have been entitled in the absence of his or her negligence and then to reduce the award by the percentage of negligence attributable to the patient, regardless of what this percentage may be. Thus, if a jury concluded that a patient was entitled to $500,000 in damages for an injury, but that negligent conduct on the part of the patient contributed to the injury by a factor of 60 percent, then the actual damage award would be reduced by $300,000, or 60 percent of the amount to which the patient would otherwise have been entitled.

Under a modified form of the comparative negligence doctrine, when a patient's negligent conduct is more than 50 percent responsible for the injury in question, the patient is barred from recovering any damages. A patient whose negligence is viewed as being less than 50 percent responsible for his or her injury is awarded damages in an amount that is reduced in accordance with the same rules that apply to the pure form of comparative negligence.

The modified comparative negligence doctrine seeks to strike a balance between the rigors of the contributory negligence doctrine and the liberality of the more patient-oriented pure comparative negligence doctrine. Determining the degree to which a patient is negligent thus has a significant potential to reduce, if not bar, a damage award.

Statutory Immunities

Various state statutes have been developed with the intent of fostering certain conduct on the part of physicians and surgeons. These statutes usually are designed to encourage physician participation in activities that further the state's interest in protecting the public health. Typically, such statutes confer immunity from potential medical malpractice liability in connection with the provision of emergency medical care, participation in peer review, disclosure of confidential medical information where significant interests of third parties are affected, and in other situations in which the risk of malpractice liability could discourage physicians from engaging in activities believed to contribute to the public good. Certain immunities also are provided under federal laws intended to accomplish similar public policy objectives.

Although a comprehensive detailing of these state and federal statutes is beyond the scope of this discussion, a brief review should suggest how they are intended to operate.

Encouraging physicians to provide emergency medical care at the scene of automobile accidents and other emergency situations has probably been the major impetus behind the enactment of state immunity legislation in the United States. Referred to as *Good Samaritan statutes*, these specify that physicians and surgeons who act in good faith to provide emergency medical care, without charging a fee, are immune from liability for acts or omissions that might otherwise have resulted in a medical malpractice damage award. This protection typically is afforded to surgeons licensed in the state in question or in any other state and is applicable so long as the surgeon is not guilty of willful and wanton misconduct, such as acting with utter indifference to or conscious disregard for the safety of another.

The courts have been increasingly inclined to construe Good Samaritan statutes quite broadly, maximizing the protection they afford. For that reason, a surgeon may not only be protected in providing emergency medical care at the scene of an event, such as a highway emergency, but even in the provision of emergency medical care without fee that takes place in a medical setting.

For example, in *Kearns v. Superior Court*, 252 Cal. Rptr. 4 (Cal. App. 1988), the court concluded that a physician who had provided emergency medical care in a hospital setting to a person who was not his patient was entitled to immunity from malpractice liability.

The *Kearns* suit arose out of an incident that occurred during surgical removal of a malignant ovarian tumor. When the surgeon performing the procedure encountered difficulties and requested immediate assistance, the request was responded to by another physician who was in the hospital at the time seeing his own patients. In the course of removing the tumor, its contents were spilled into the patient's abdomen, seeding it with cancer cells. The patient subsequently brought suit against both the surgeon and the physician who responded to the call for emergency assistance.

Relying on provisions of the California Good Samaritan law, the assisting physician moved for summary judgment. When the trial judge denied this motion, the physician successfully sought an order from the California Court of Appeals directing the judge to grant the motion. Noting that the situation had indeed constituted an emergency, the appeals court observed that previous California court decisions had applied the Good Samaritan statute to hospital situations and affirmed the propriety of applying the statute in such a case. "[I]t is in the best interests of the public that the Good Samaritan laws be applied in a manner which encourages a physician who happens to be in the hospital and available to provide intraoperative assistance when unexpected complications arise during surgery to provide the assistance requested," the court stated. Such judicial reasoning also has been followed in other jurisdictions, especially when the surgeon in question has acted in an emergency and without receiving a fee for the Good Samaritan services rendered.

Fostering the involvement of surgeons in medical peer review contributes to ensuring the quality of health care. Some physicians, however, have legitimate concerns about potential liability for libel, slander, or defamation of character and other liability that could arise from participation in the process. Such concerns have tended to have a chilling effect on the willingness of medical professionals to participate in peer review. In response, state legislatures have enacted statutes that encourage physicians and surgeons to serve on, or otherwise provide service to, peer review or other committees whose purpose is to improve or benefit patient care or otherwise reduce morbidity and mortality rates.

The mechanism used to encourage such involvement is statutory immunity from civil or criminal prosecution. Surgeons are thereby encouraged not only to participate in the peer review process, but to offer frank and candid discussion of the quality of medical care provided by their peers.

On the federal level, the Health Care Quality Improvement Act of 1986 also provides physician immunity from antitrust and other civil liability in certain situations involving good faith participation in the peer review process.

Statutory immunity involving disclosure of information acquired in the physician-patient relationship that might otherwise be deemed confidential also has been provided in the interest of protecting the public health. For example, a surgeon who, in good faith, reports a suspected incident of child abuse or neglect generally is immune from civil or criminal liability that might otherwise have resulted from disclosure of information acquired in the physician-patient relationship. Similarly, state statutes that require physicians to disclose sexually transmitted disease or information relating to injury reasonably believed to have been caused by discharge of a firearm or other involvement in criminal activity also provide immunity from civil liability.

Reporting information that may protect an innocent third party from serious physical injury also may be encouraged by state statutes. For example, some state mental health laws provide immunity to physicians who disclose confidential health information in situations in which disclosure is necessary to protect a third party from a clear and imminent risk of serious physical injury.

In all, a diverse array of state and federal statutory provisions have been enacted to provide immunity to physicians and surgeons in connection with the kind of conduct deemed to advance public health objectives. These statutes often provide immunity from professional disciplinary action by the state medical licensing board as well. Surgeons whose alleged medical malpractice may involve conduct that is protected under a statute or governmental regulation should examine whether the allegedly negligent conduct may be immune from liability, because such immunities can provide an excellent mechanism for disposing of medical malpractice litigation.

Efforts to Reform and Change

Tort Reform

The inadequacies of the tort system have increasingly come to be recognized. As a result, most state legislatures have attempted to institute some form of tort reform, particularly for, but not necessarily limited to, medical malpractice. Two major waves of tort reform have occurred, the first in response to the malpractice crisis of the 1970s, the second during the malpractice crisis of the 1980s. These legislative reforms included changes in the legal rules of the tort system, the most commonly understood application of the term tort reform. Because the availability and affordability of adequate liability insurance were major issues raised in these crises, as were medical practice patterns and adequate provider quality assurance, reform legislation also has resulted in the modification of insurance practices.

Responses to problems related to the availability of insurance and its cost include the creation of new sources of insurance, among them, state-operated compensation funds, joint underwriting associations, and physician-owned insurance companies, as well as changes in the kinds of policies that are offered. Problems related to provider practice patterns have been addressed by programs for quality assurance and risk management, although it is as yet unclear what long-term effects such widely implemented programs will have on the malpractice problem.

Reform Measures

State legislatures have taken a piecemeal approach to the professional liability problem, enacting more than 20 specific types of legal rule changes in the interest of tort reform. These reforms vary considerably from state to state, but, as a general rule, fall into three categories: those that affect the initiation of claims, those that affect the standard of care and proof of its breach, and those that affect the amount recoverable in a malpractice suit. These reforms include:

Elimination of the Ad Damnum Clause The *ad damnum clause* refers to the statement of the amount of damages sought in a plaintiff's claim. Because publication of these amounts may generate unfavorable publicity, harm a defendant's reputation, and perhaps influence a jury, many states have prohibited inclusion of the clause in a pleading or permit only a statement that damages exceed a certain specified amount.

Requirement of Arbitration Under reforms enacted in various states, this method of nonjudicial resolution of a controversy by a neutral third party may be elected by agreement (voluntary) or may be imposed by law (mandatory). Also, the resolution suggested may be binding or nonbinding. The advantages arbitration offers are fewer forms to fill out, greater privacy for the parties, faster resolution of claims, lower cost, and perhaps the availability of a higher level of technical expertise to evaluate a claim. Although arbitration has been used with a great deal of success in commercial and labor disputes, its use in resolving medical claims has not yet been studied enough to establish it as the procedure of choice.

Regulation of Attorneys' Fees The contingent fee, the most common arrangement for payment of plaintiff attorneys in malpractice cases, allocates to the attorney a predetermined percentage of any final award or settlement, usually in addition to expenses of litigation. If the plaintiff loses, the attorney receives no fee. Defense attorney fees are usually billed on an hourly basis. Regulation of plaintiff attorney fees, which has been effected in some states, may consist of establishing a sliding scale to determine the percentage of the award that may be paid to the attorney, limiting the fee to a certain percentage of the total award, or requiring court determination or approval of a reasonable fee. Proponents of attorney fee regulation argue that it would allocate more funds to the injured party, reduce nonmeritorious claims, and encourage earlier settlement. Opponents view the contingent fee as "the key to the courthouse" for claimants and as a screening mechanism that encourages attorneys to eliminate claims that are unlikely to result in recovery of damages.

Modification of the Collateral Source Rule Traditionally, this rule has prevented a jury from considering evidence concerning payments to the injured party from other sources, including private health or disability insurance, workers' compensation, and governmental benefit payments. Advocating modification or abolishment of the rule, proponents of this form of reform maintain that recovery from multiple sources provides an unwarranted windfall for claimants and contributes to the high cost of malpractice litigation. The rule has been modified in a number of states to reduce duplicate payments for medical malpractice, either by permitting the jury to be informed about such payments or by mandating that the amounts of some or all of any collateral benefits be deducted from awards resulting from the malpractice claim.

Improved Data Collection and Processing The unavailability of reliable data has been a major impediment to objective evaluation and resolution of the medical professional liability problem. Some reform efforts have therefore provided for data reporting and processing programs, which have focused on provider disciplinary procedures and insurance factors. Responsibility for data collection is most commonly vested in state licensing authorities, state insurance departments, or the recently activated, federally mandated National Practitioner Data Bank.

Establishment of Expert Witness Qualifications Expert witnesses play a crucial role in medical malpractice cases, a fact that raises important concerns about the qualification and regulation of paid experts, especially those who testify for the plaintiff. Legislation in several states has established minimum qualifications for expert witnesses, such as requiring an expert to have devoted at least half of his or her time within the preceding two-year period to actual clinical practice in the same profession as the defendant, requiring the expert witness to have a current license to practice in the same or a related specialty as the defendant, or requiring the witness to have spent a substantial portion of time in actual clinical practice in the same or a related specialty.

Passage of Frivolous Claim Provisions Several states have passed legislation to discourage nonmeritorious malpractice claims. Such statutes may involve requiring the plaintiff to reimburse the defendant for attorney fees, witness fees, and other costs; requiring an expert affidavit or certificate of merit as a prerequisite to filing a claim; requiring a plaintiff to post a bond to initiate a claim; or permitting a defendant to file an affidavit of noninvolvement in the lawsuit, permitting expeditious dismissal from the case.

Clarification of Informed Consent Requirements Disclosures required under the informed consent doctrine vary from state to state, making it difficult for health care providers to comply with them. Proponents of reform advocate legislation to clarify what and how much information providers must disclose to satisfy this requirement.

Itemization of Jury Verdicts Although juries deliberate upon the individual components of a lawsuit, such as the plaintiff's past and future medical expenses, past and future income loss, past and future pain and suffering, or other nonpecuniary losses, common law verdicts traditionally are rendered in lump sums. Proponents of reform argue for itemization of amounts awarded in malpractice cases in the interest of encouraging realistic assessments of losses and more objective awards, as well as to permit more effective subsequent analysis of verdicts.

Limitations on Joint and Several Liability Except where it has been changed by state statute, the present law holds each defendant named in a lawsuit "jointly and severally liable," a statement that means that each is responsible for paying the full cost of a plaintiff's award. Under this system, the defendant with the most resources—or the one who, in legal terminology, is said to have the "deep pocket"—may bear the greatest share of the damage award, even though having played only a marginal role in causing the injury. This has led to abusive litigation practices, such as "shotgun tactics," under which those with assets or insurance may be named as defendants in a lawsuit, even though they have no readily apparent responsibility for the injury. The practice also creates serious problems for insurers, who must project costs and determine the price of insurance. In response, a number of states have passed *comparative negligence* legislation, which generally limits a defendant's responsibility to payment of that defendant's portion of the fault.

Limitations on Statutes of Limitation Some states' statutes of limitation permit a plaintiff significant time in which to initiate a suit, presenting major problems for insurers in establishing rates and reserves and for defendants in producing evidence and witnesses. These problems are compounded by the doctrines of discovery and continuing treatment, which may toll the statutes until injury is discovered or reasonably should have been discovered, or until a patient is no longer under treatment. In some states, reforms of these statutes have been enacted, shortening the time in which a lawsuit must be filed after an injury occurs, is discovered, or should be discovered, and analyses indicate that reducing statutes of limitation in this way effectively decreases the frequency of malpractice claims.

Limitations on Liability Placing caps on the amounts of awards, either by limiting the total amounts that may be recovered or, more commonly, limiting awards for such noneconomic damages as pain and suffering, has been the most effective method of reducing the severity of claims, according to currently available data. By 1987, a total of 30 states had passed legislation to limit the liability of health care providers and others. Although this legislation has been subjected to extensive constitutional challenge and some statutes have been struck down, others have survived, including statutes presently in place in California and Indiana.

Implementation of Periodic Payment Schedules Judgments and settlements in civil litigation, such as malpractice litigation, are traditionally awarded in a lump sum. Proponents of reform advocate periodic or structured payments, which can result in significant savings for defendants and insurers by reducing the total cost of awards. Further cost reductions may be realized through provisions for modifying an award if a plaintiff recovers from the injury or dies unexpectedly. From the claimant's point of view, the mechanism provides certainty of payment over a period of time and avoids the possibility of mismanagement of the initial lump sum.

Establishment of Pretrial Screening Panels Medical review panels for pretrial screening of claims are intended to discourage nonmeritorious claims and encourage the expeditious settlement of others. Proponents of screening hope that panel decisions will reduce the number of claims that go to trial. However, opponents argue that screening adds an additional and perhaps ineffective step to the litigation process, while providing an opportunity for plaintiff attorneys to better educate themselves about the matters at issue and for plaintiffs to reap the benefit of inexpensive expert testimony. Nor do they believe that there has been much evidence to date of the effectiveness of screening in reducing the frequency of claims.

Elimination of Punitive Damages Punitive or, as they are sometimes termed, exemplary damages have been carried over from the criminal law into the law of torts and may be awarded if a wrongdoer's acts have been deliberate, intentional, or otherwise outrageous. Such behavior is generally associated with crime and is seldom a component in the unintentional acts on which negligence actions are based. Opponents of reform emphasize the potential deterrent value of punitive damages and their role in reimbursing the actual expenses of litigation, which are not otherwise recoverable by a plaintiff. Proponents of reform contend that allegations of extreme behavior are frequently used inappropriately in liability cases as bargaining chips for settlement purposes, further maintaining that review by institutions or provider licensing boards or resort to the criminal justice system are more appropriate methods for resolving questions of gross professional misconduct.

Prohibition or Clarification of the *Res Ipsa Loquitur* Doctrine As previously noted, citation of this legal doctrine shifts the burden of proof from the plaintiff to the defendant, requiring the defendant to show that the injury did not result from the defendant's negligence. Although application of the doctrine was expanded in the early 1970s, it does not appear to be a major factor in malpractice litigation at present. Expanded application places malpractice defendants at a disadvantage, inasmuch as medically caused injuries, although sometimes difficult to account for, are not always the result of provider negligence. Reform legislation, passed by several states, may prohibit use of the doctrine, codify it, or otherwise clarify the circumstances under which it applies.

Establishment of Study Commissions for Professional Liability The establishment of such bodies has been a feature of tort reform efforts in a number of states. Study commissions are frequently appointed by the governor and typically are made up of insurance commissioners, legislators, providers, consumers, and others. As a general rule, they are charged with reviewing and making recommendations on the professional liability situation in their states.

Other Reforms of Legal Rules A number of other approaches to tort reform have been at least considered, among them, provision that a breach of contract must be documented by a written and properly executed document, that notice of the intent to sue be made a prerequisite to initiating litigation, and that expressions of humane concern be inadmissible in the establishment of liability. Minimum rules for jury instructions regarding the standard of care also may be established or revised, and physicians' countersuits may be facilitated by eliminating the requirement that they must demonstrate that the physician was actually damaged as a result of the original suit.

Measures of Success

Although both the 1970s and 1980s malpractice crises abated after each wave of reforms, the complex and cyclical nature of the malpractice problem, the variations in reform packages, and the lack of adequate data make it difficult to evaluate the real effects of tort reforms, even now. Nor are the specific effects of individual reforms easy to quantitate. Meaningful assessment is further complicated by frequent challenges to the constitutionality of the various reforms, delaying their implementation or ultimately reversing them in a number of states. The results of the statistical analyses that are available are equivocal in indicating their effectiveness, or suggest that they are ineffective in reducing the frequency and severity of claims. Nor do specific reforms correlate with decreased insurance premiums.

Nevertheless, tort reforms do appear to have moderated and improved the malpractice climate in several states, most notably California and Indiana, where legislative reforms have been implemented and subsequently upheld. That experience, the available analyses, and expert opinions all indicate that the three methods of reform that appear statistically to be most effective in reducing either the frequency or severity of claims are placing caps on awards, modifying the collateral source rule to reduce

II / Substantive Tort Law

awards by amounts payable by collateral sources, and shortening statutes of limitation. Although arbitration does appear to reduce the severity of claims, that fact probably is due to an increase in the frequency of small claims. The periodic payment of awards and elimination of joint and several liability can be expected to decrease insurance costs, and are otherwise beneficial.

Efforts to Change

Despite all of the tort reform efforts of the past 15 years, it seems clear that the system of dealing with medical injury in the United States is not working. Physicians continue to suffer severe emotional distress as a result of being sued, even when they are eventually acquitted by the courts. Access and quality of health care are being negatively affected. The cost of defensive medicine continues to escalate. Fewer than one percent of patients who experience an adverse event during the course of medical treatment ever receive compensation for their injury. And professional liability premiums remain an unbearable expense for many practicing physicians.

Looking to the future, it is apparent that some means other than tort mechanisms must be found to provide hope for all those who now are so poorly served by the system currently in place. Several methods of alternative dispute resolution (ADR) are discussed.

The Fault-Based Administrative Alternative

In 1988, the American Medical Association, 31 national medical specialty societies, including the American College of Surgeons, and the Council of Medical Specialty Societies launched the AMA/Specialty Society Project. The primary objective of this joint project is to develop an alternative to the present system of resolving medical liability disputes. Under this alternative system, such disputes would be adjudicated by an expert administrative agency, which could be either a new agency or one that represented a modification of the existing state licensing board. This medical board would also have the power to take appropriate action to identify and rehabilitate or discipline physicians whose practice patterns pose a threat to patients. This plan, described below, has not yet been implemented by any state.

The administrative system for adjudicating medical liability would provide for an initial review of claims, a hearing before an expert hearing examiner, an appeal to a medical board panel, and a further appeal to a state appellate court.

Under proposed prehearing procedures, medical board claims reviewers would quickly evaluate claims and dismiss those without merit. Claims that survived this initial review would then be submitted by the claims reviewers to an expert in the same field as the health care provider involved in the matter. The expert would review the claim and decide whether or not it had merit. The claims reviewers also would assist the patient in evaluating the claim and any settlement offers.

If a claim was not settled in this way, it would be assigned to one of the medical board's hearing examiners. To encourage reasonable and timely settlements, both parties would be required to submit blind (sealed) settlement offers prior to a hearing, and both would be subject to sanctions if the eventual outcome of the case did not represent an improvement over a settlement offer that the party had rejected. The hearing examiner also would be responsible for assuring that the discovery phase of litigation was handled expeditiously and that both parties had valid expert evidence available to support their case.

At the hearing itself, the examiner would have broad authority to conduct the proceedings, including authority to call an independent expert to provide assistance in deciding the case. The hearing examiner would be required to render a written decision within 90 days of the hearing, specifying whether the health care provider was liable for the claimant's injury and, if so, the size of the damage award.

II / Substantive Tort Law

A hearing examiner's decision could be appealed to the medical board. If the appeal was determined to be valid, the board would have the discretion to award fees and costs incurred in the appeal. The medical board would hear these cases as an appellate body in three-member panels, making completely independent determinations of whether or not the health care provider's conduct was inadequate and caused the claimant's injury. A further level to which the parties could appeal the medical board's decision would be the intermediate appellate court of the state, where the review would be limited to whether the board acted contrary to statute or to its own rules. The entire procedure can be diagramed as follows:

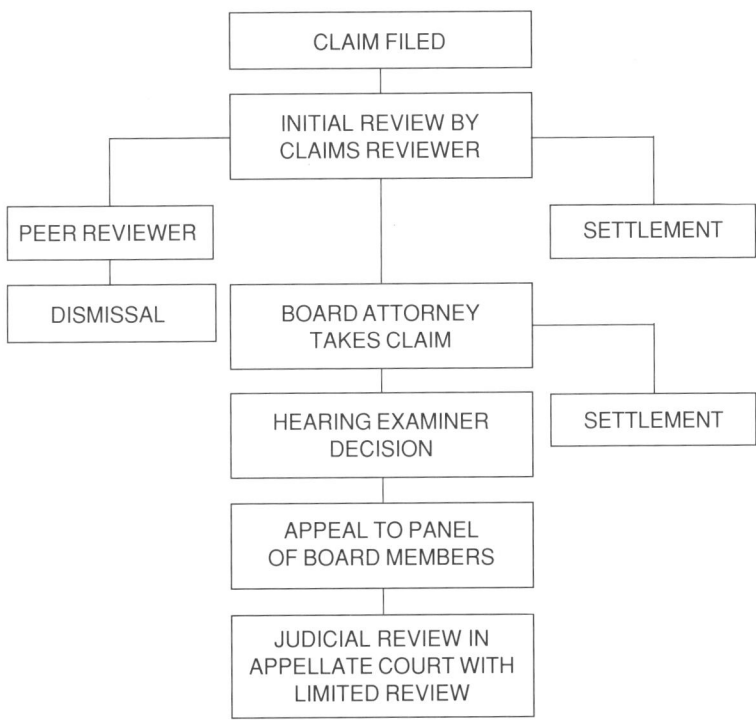

In addition to acting as an adjudicator of medical liability claims, the medical board also would develop rules and substantive guidelines to complement the statutory standards, and would have administrative authority to initiate rule-making and to solicit public comments. A rule promulgated by the board would have the force of law and be subject to judicial review by an appellate court to determine if it were arbitrary, capricious, or in excess of the medical board's authority.

Existing medical boards would, of course, have to be restructured in order to perform the complex and sensitive functions required under this proposed system. The board's performance-monitoring function also would be strengthened. Alternately, a new agency would have to be created. The board would consist of full-time members selected by the state's governor and approved by its legislature. The AMA/Specialty Society project recommends that it consist of seven members, at least two, but no more than three, of whom would be physicians.

Implementation of this administrative model would require substantial funding, and the use of general revenues would be necessary. The state could also raise initial funding through assessments against insurers, physicians, and other health care providers.

The major advantages the system would offer physicians, project authors say, are certainty and predictability in liability determinations and, ultimately, in professional premiums. Other advantages include placing the adjudication of liability in the hands of expert reviewers armed with clear guidelines, placing caps on awards for damages, and reducing the length of the adjudicatory process. The key benefit for patients would be to ensure them the right to a hearing without having to find and pay a lawyer.

One disadvantage to the proposal is that it would give the medical board wide powers to define the practice standards under which a claim for medical liability would be established, as well as enhanced powers to monitor physicians' performance, including, but not limited to, the power to require periodic physician performance reviews by insurers, hospitals, and other health care institutions. Another major objection is that the proposal would perpetuate the complex, expensive, and inefficient necessity of establishing fault, which can be so damaging to the physician.

The Contractual Approach

The use of *contracts between individuals* (private contracts) to resolve disputes and allocate risk is another possible approach to solving the tort law problem. Past attempts by medical care providers to implement this concept have usually been struck down by the courts on the grounds that it violates public policy. However, pretreatment contracts between patients and physicians might be used to specify the standard of care, perhaps by defining the physician's duty as being to perform as "a reasonable and prudent physician." Given concerns about the cost of health care, a duty to provide cost-effective care might also be included in this definition.

Another way in which a contract could be used would be to define appropriate credentials for expert witnesses or mandate the use of impartial experts in the event of litigation. Still another contractual option might be to redefine liability, using gross negligence rather than ordinary negligence as the standard.

While contractual limitations may hold some promise, they also raise questions regarding their practicality, given the time, uncertainty, and cost of proceeding through the court system to defend the constitutional challenges to them that are certain to arise. Indeed, the magnitude of the professional liability problem today may well make this approach too impractical, too time-consuming, and too costly to be seriously considered.

The Early Offer and Recovery System

For many years, Jeffrey O'Connell of the University of Virginia has advocated an *early offer and recovery* system as an alternative to currently available approaches. He writes:

Under the proposed law, the alleged perpetrator of a tort would have the option of offering to pay the claimant's net economic loss, in periodic payments as incurred. The offer would have to be made within 180 days of the claim (a short period, compared with the duration of a tort case).

If a defendant made this offer of prompt payment of economic loss, under the proposed law, the claimant would in most cases be forced to accept it and would be foreclosed from further pursuit of a tort claim. There are two exceptions in which a plaintiff could refuse the offer and pursue the normal course of tort litigation. One would be if the defendant intentionally caused the injury. The other would be if the victim's economic losses were minimal.

The settlement offer, to be binding, would have to cover all medical expenses (including rehabilitation) and wage losses not already covered by "collateral sources" like health or disability insurance. This collateral-source offset reflects the proposal's focus not so much on punishment as on insurance; its chief aim is to compensate those who need it most rather than to penalize fault. For like reasons, the settlement offer would have to provide a reasonable hourly fee for the claimant's lawyer, including reasonable expenses and cost of obtaining legal advice about the offer itself. This provision is necessary to ensure that injured victims recoup the full amount of their out-of-pocket loss. Requiring victims to pay these costs would force them to subtract unavoidable and sometimes sizable outlays from their recovery of economic loss. Under the present tort system, attorney's fees are often paid out of noneconomic damages, and juries are often thought to boost the amount of noneconomic recovery they award to cover these fees.

The proposal, however, would not require any defendant to make such a settlement offer. Such a requirement would place unmanageable new burdens on defendants and encourage baseless suits. If no such offer were made, the current tort system, including recovery for noneconomic losses, would be available to injured victims.

Although it would represent a definite improvement over the current method, O'Connell's proposed solution would create a whole new set of issues and complexities for the practicing physician. Physicians would have to decide whether they were a perpetrator of a tort or if the incident was a maloccurrence. If it were a maloccurrence, would the next step be a potential court trial, with its attendant publicity and emotional trauma for the physician and his or her family? Would physicians wish to risk their careers and financial future on the ability of a lay jury to understand a complex medical case? And if a physician offered to settle a claim, what penalties would the professional liability insurer, the Board of Registration, and the National Practitioner Data Bank impose? Because of these uncertainties, it is unlikely that this proposal would be universally adopted and applied by physicians.

The No-fault Patient Compensation Model

Under the *no-fault compensation* plan, in return for waiving tort claims, a patient could receive compensation for a maloccurrence without having to prove that the physician was at fault. This approach would ensure legitimate claimants prompt compensation for injuries resulting from medical maloccurrences. This plan would be voluntary, so a patient could elect to forgo the plan and use the tort system to obtain relief.

To implement it, a corporation would have to be created to administer a system of benefits for compensable medical injuries. Such a corporation would probably be governed, and its corporate power exercised, by a board of directors composed of physicians, insurers, and consumers. Members would be appointed by the state's governor and approved by its legislature.

A compensable medical injury would be defined as any illness, injury, or impairment or death that either was the result of an act or failure to act by a health care provider during the course of medical examination or intervention and was not within the reasonable range of medical outcomes that may have occurred as a result of a condition, or was not, but reasonably should have been, discovered in the course of a medical examination. Medical injuries that would be excluded from coverage would be those caused primarily by a defective drug or device used in medical examination or intervention, and intentionally inflicted medical injury.

The corporation would convene boards of physician specialists in separate medical disciplines to assist it in distinguishing compensable from noncompensable medical injuries on the basis of these criteria. A list of approved compensable medical injuries would be published.

Patients could file their own claims, or physicians or hospitals could file claims on behalf of their patients. Although lawyers could also represent patients before the commission, their fees would be set statutorily, eliminating the contingency fee. The commission would award net economic loss only and structure payouts for losses extending over 90 days.

No benefits could be paid in compensation of claims for pain and suffering, mental anguish, punitive or exemplary damages, or all other general damages, as distinguished from special damages (see Glossary for definition of terms), including loss of consortium, society, companionship, control, protection, marital care, attention, advice, counsel, training, guidance, and education.

A subcommittee of the commission composed of physician specialists and perhaps called a Medical Professional Review Board would review all claims that could result in compensation in excess of $100,000. It would also investigate hospitals and physicians that were subject to repeated claims. Working in cooperation with the State Board of Registration and medical specialty societies, this board could arrange for appropriate reeducation, retraining, or disciplinary action. If a hospital was found to be substandard, the board would work with the state's hospital regulatory agency and the Joint Commission on Accreditation of Healthcare Organizations to effect corrective action.

The no-fault plan is voluntary, so the patient could elect to resort to the tort system to obtain relief. The courts, however, would be unlikely to significantly exceed the established criteria for compensation. Also, the tort route promises only a 20 percent chance of success, because defendant physicians prevail 80 percent of the time in court trials, as well as a reduction of more than 50 percent in any award for fees and expenses and a wait of up to seven years to resolve the claim.

The no-fault approach would provide the medical profession and public with comprehensive information about poor results and errors in medical practice. The issue of determining optimal treatments is one of paramount importance in the United States, where efforts to control the cost of health care are beginning to focus on preferred forms of therapy, using patient care algorithms, outcome assessments, and so on. In Sweden, the national insurance company is currently undertaking a major effort to identify preferred therapies, using data on maloccurrences from its no-fault insurance plan. Comparative data on the results of various diagnostic and treatment methods might be provided in a similar way in the United States.

Funding and Cost Considerations Funding a no-fault plan could be achieved in a variety of ways, as long as it included all individuals at risk. For example, the program could be funded by a surcharge on every health and accident policy sold, or a tax on all employers and self-employed persons, or a surcharge on state and federal income tax, or from general state and federal government revenues. While a surcharge on every major medical health and accident policy would appear preferable, it is clear that a patient compensation system which covers all medical maloccurrences cannot be funded solely by physicians, who constitute less than 0.2 percent of the population.

Because more patients would receive compensation under a no-fault system, a justifiable concern is whether its cost would exceed that of the present tort system. The answer to that question probably is no. First, transaction costs (overhead) would be reduced significantly, resulting in from 50 percent or more of the total cost of litigation to less than 10 percent, leaving far more money to be redirected to patients. Second, a no-fault system would compensate a patient only for actual economic losses. Finally, it would substantially reduce the enormous costs now associated with physicians' need to practice defensive medicine.

Although it is difficult to estimate the exact cost of a compensatory system without a list of compensable events, some indirect evidence can be obtained from the experience of others. A recent Harvard University Medical Practice Study of more than 30,000 hospitalized patients revealed that a no-fault system would cost no more than our current system. A statistical review of 100 closed claims by the Kentucky Medical Insurance Company compared the cost of pursing those claims under the current tort system with costs that would be incurred under a proposed patient compensation system. The study indicated that a savings of almost 50 percent would have been achieved under a patient compensation system, while the injured parties would have received greater net benefits than under the tort system.

Both Sweden and New Zealand currently have in place long-standing, successful no-fault medical injury systems. New Zealand introduced the first comprehensive no-fault compensation system for personal injury due to accidents in 1974. The system covers medical mishaps and malpractice, as well as traffic, home, and sporting accidents. The categories it covers are medical, surgical, dental, and first aid misadventures; actual bodily harm, including pregnancy and mental or nervous shock suffered by one person as a result of an act of aggression by another; incapacity resulting from an occupational disease or industrial deafness; and the physical and mental consequences of personal injury by accident.

The New Zealand Accident Compensation Corporation is funded by general tax funds, employers' contributions, and a levy on the self-employed. Compensation is made in the form of lump sums for loss of function and continuing payments based on earnings before the accident. A claimant who is dissatisfied with the amount of compensation may appeal first to the corporation, then to the courts. The right to go to court is lost, however, when compensation is accepted.

Sweden introduced its no-fault medical injury system on January 1, 1975. The key to compensation under the Swedish system is an injury or illness that "has occurred as a direct consequence of examination, treatment, or any other similar procedure which does not constitute an unavoidable complication of an act justified from a medical point of view." Some broad exclusions are provided for, including infections resulting from failure to use sterile instruments or substances; drug-related injuries, which are covered under a separate insurance plan; unavoidable results of illness or surgery, such as surgical scars; and failure to diagnose.

To recover damages in the case of infections and failure to diagnose, patients must prove negligence under the Swedish tort system. Once negligence is proved, compensation is made through a patient insurance program. Guidelines for determining which events are compensable were promulgated with the assistance of the medical profession.

Both the New Zealand and Swedish systems appear to be working well. Both are efficient, fair, and cost-effective. The Swedish system operates at a cost of just over two dollars per citizen per year.

In the United States, three programs provide examples of how the no-fault concept has been applied in response to crises that arose as a result of the American way of dealing with professional liability claims.

The National Vaccine Injury Compensation Program, a federal no-fault compensation program for children injured in vaccine-related incidents, was created under P.L. 99-660, which was enacted in 1986 after the only three companies still manufacturing childhood vaccines informed the federal government that they could no longer continue to do so in the face of their vulnerability to tort liability. P.L. 99-660 and its funding component, P.L. 100-203, covers all victims of injuries caused by childhood vaccinations without requiring proof of fault. In the event of a claim, all related expenses are covered for the life of the injured patient, up to a limit of $30,000. The program is funded by an excise tax levied on every dose of vaccine sold.

In February 1987, the state of Virginia enacted a compensation system for infants severely injured at birth. The Injured Infants Act, which was drafted by the Medical Society of Virginia, created a separate system that would compensate "profoundly injured babies whose injuries are birth-related and not due to genetic or congenital abnormalities." The amount of awards is determined and granted by the state Industrial Commission. The program is funded by assessments of $250 per year on all physicians in the state, $5,000 on participating obstetricians, $50 per delivery on participating hospitals, and 0.25 percent of net premiums on liability carriers operating in the state.

In Florida, an Injured Infants Plan was enacted in February 1988 as part of a larger package of legislative reforms that included voluntary arbitration systems, immunity for physicians treating patients in emergency rooms, increased funds to expand the state Department of Professional Regulation, and an optional no-fault plan to compensate infants who suffer birth-related neurologic injuries. Funding is achieved through levies of $5,000 on participating obstetricians, $250 on all other physicians, and $50 per birth on hospitals. Other funds come from fees paid to the state by insurers and others.

It is clear that, when faced with a crisis in access to care, informed legislators are quick to recognize no-fault plans as a meaningful solution. By removing the claims process from the courtroom, this approach eliminates the costly, inefficient, and difficult necessity of establishing fault and separates the two disparate issues of compensating those patients who suffer a maloccurrence from the need to identify and discipline physicians whose practice is substandard.

A patient compensation plan (no-fault) recently received a major boost when the prestigious American Law Institute published a two-volume report, *Enterprise Responsibility for Personal Injury*, on April 15, 1991. In its conclusion on medical liability, the report states:

> We are persuaded of two related judgments about no-fault liability accidents: First, the no-fault model should be considered a serious and plausible alternative in the ongoing debate about how best to deal with medical injuries. Second, medical no-fault can and should be introduced initially only on a voluntary, elective basis.

Summary

Professional liability continues to be one of the most severe problems facing practicing physicians today, and one that adversely affects access, quality, and cost of health care in the United States. More than any other consideration, it dictates how physicians practice medicine, from undertreating patients with cancer to overtreating pregnant women. It influences which cases physicians will accept, the diagnostic studies they will perform, and the types of treatments they will administer. Professional liability is forcing physicians to practice medicine defensively, adding significantly to the already rising cost of health care, while adversely affecting the training of future physicians and those who aspire to careers in medicine.

The existing tort system is unfair, untimely, and inefficient, and fails to benefit those it is intended to protect. Remedial legislation, which has been tried unsuccessfully in this country since 1975, obviously is not the total answer to the problem. We must have a major change in our tort system which removes the entire process from the courtroom so that maloccurrences are covered by some form of alternative dispute resolution (ADR) before any further damage occurs to the quality of our health care and the physicians who provide it.

Bibliography

Abraham KS: Medical liability reform, a conceptual framework. *JAMA*, 260:68-72, 1988.

American College of Legal Medicine: *Legal Medicine—Legal Dynamics of Medical Encounters*. St. Louis: CV Mosby Company, 1988.

American Law Institute: *Reporter's Study on Enterprise Responsibility for Personal Injury*. Philadelphia: American Law Institute, 1991.

American Medical Association/Specialty Society Medical Liability Project: A proposed alternative to the civil justice system for resolving medical liability disputes. A fault-based administrative system. American Medical Association/Specialty Society Medical Liability Project, January 13, 1988.

Atiyah PS: *Accidents, Compensation, and the Law*. London: Weidenfeld and Nicolson, 1980.

Blair AP: *Accident Compensation in New Zealand*, ed 2. Wellington, New Zealand: Butterworth, 1983.

Bowen OR, Burke TR: New directions in effective quality of care: Patient outcome research. *Fed Am Health Syst Rev*: 50-53, September/October 1988.

Brahams D: The Swedish medical insurance schemes: The way ahead for the United Kingdom? *Lancet*, 1:43-47, 1988.

Bullock F: *Law Relating to Medical, Dental and Veterinarian Practice*. London: Bailliere, Tindall and Cox, 1929.

Burns CR: Malpractice suits in American medicine before the Civil War. *Bull Hist Med*, 43(1):42, 1969.

Cohen E, Korper S: The Swedish no-fault patient compensation program: Provisions and preliminary findings. *Ins Law J*, 637:7-80, 1976.

Cooper JK: Sweden's no-fault patient-injury insurance. *N Engl J Med*, 294(23):1268-1270, 1976.

Cosman MP: The medieval medical third party: Compulsory consultation and malpractice insurance. *Ann Plast Surg*, 8:152, 1982.

Dias RWM, Markesinis BS: *Tort Law*. Oxford: Clarendon Press, 1984.

Dobbs DB, et al: *Prosser and Keeton on the Law of Torts* (Pocket Part). St. Paul, MN: West Publishing Co, 1988.

Elwell JJ: *A Medico-Legal Treatise on Malpractice and Medical Evidence*. New York: Baker, Voorhis and Company, Publishers, 1866.

Ellwood PM: Shattuck lecture—Outcomes management: A technology of patient experience. *N Engl J Med*, 318(23):1549-1556, 1988.

Epstein RA: Medical malpractice: The case for contract. *ABF Res J*, 87:150, 1976.

Fleming JG: *An Introduction to the Law of Torts*. Oxford: Clarendon Press, 1985.

Hall MA, Ellman IM: *Health Care Law and Ethics*. St. Paul, MN: West Publishing Co, 1990.

Halley MM, Fowks RJ, et al: A medical accident compensation system: A model act. *Kansas Med*, 89(10):259-282, 1988.

Halley MM, Fowks RJ, Bigler FC, Ryan DL (eds): *Medical Malpractice Solutions: Systems and Proposals for Injury Compensation*. Springfield, IL: Charles C Thomas, 1989.

Harvard University: *Patients, Doctors, and Lawyers: Medical Injury, Malpractice Litigation, and Patient Compensation in New York. A Report of the Harvard Medical Practice Study to the State of New York, 1990*. Cambridge, MA: University of Harvard, 1990.

Havighurst CC: Private reform of tort-law dogma: Market opportunities and legal obstacles. *Law Contemp Prob*, 49(2):143-172, 1986.

Havighurst CC, Tancredi LR: Medical adversity insurance—A no-fault approach to medical malpractice and quality assurance. *Milbank Mem Fund Q Health Soc*, 51(2):125-168, 1973.

Health C: How Abraham Lincoln dealt with a malpractice suit [letter to the editor]. *N Engl J Med*, 295:735, 1976.

Keeton, WP, et al: *Prosser and Keeton on Torts*, ed 5. St. Paul, MN: West Publishing Co, 1984.

King JH: *The Law of Medical Malpractice*. St. Paul, MN: West Publishing Co, 1986.

Manuel BM: Is tort reform the answer? An alternative approach to end the malpractice crisis. *Mass Med* 2:42, 1987.

Moran PT: The New Zealand experience of no-fault compensation. *Med-Leg J*, 53(pt 4):222-224, 1985.

O'Connell J: Neo-no-fault: A fair-exchange proposal for tort reform. In Olson W (ed): *New Directions in Liability Laws*. New York: Academy of Political Science, 1988.

O'Connell J: Offers that can't be refused: Foreclosure of personal injury claims by defendant's prompt tender of claimant's net economic losses. *Northwestern U Law Rev*, 77:589-632, 1982.

Oldertz C: *Compensation for Personal Injuries. The Swedish Patient and Pharma Insurance*. Stockholm, Sweden: Pharma Insurance, January 16, 1989.

Oldertz C: Security insurance, patient insurance, and pharmaceutical insurance in Sweden. *Am J Comp Law*, 34:635-656, 1986.

Relman AS: Assessment and accountability: The third revolution in medical care. *N Engl J Med*, 319:1220-1222, 1988.

Robinson GO: Rethinking the allocation of medical malpractice risks between patients and providers. *Law Contemp Prob*, 49(2):173-199, 1986.

Roper WF, et al: Effectiveness in health care: An initiative to evaluate and improve medical practice. *N Engl J Med*, 319:1172-1202, 1988.

Royal Commission of Inquiry of New Zealand: *Compensation for Personal Injury in New Zealand: Report of the Royal Commission of Inquiry*. Wellington, New Zealand: AR Shearer, Government Printer, December 1967.

Sandor AA: The history of professional liability suits in the United States. *JAMA*, 163:459, 1957.

Schneider WR: *The Law of Workmen's Compensation*, ed 2. St. Louis: Thomas Law Books, 1932.

Skandia Insurance Company, Ltd, Patient Insurance Coordination Group: *Injury Prevention Activities within the Patient Insurance*. Stockholm, Sweden: The Patient Insurance Coordination Group of Skandia Insurance Company, Ltd, June 1, 1989.

Spencer FC: The expert witness: One surgeon's opinion. *Bull Am Coll Surg*, 73(5): 11-140, 1988.

Stallybrass WTS: *Salmond's Law of Torts*, ed 10. London: Sweet and Maxwell, 1945.

Tancredi LD: Designing a no-fault alternative. *Law Contemp Prob*, 49:277-281, 1986.

II / Substantive Tort Law

Wedekind CL: An alternate proposal for compensating injuries occurring in the health care delivery system. *J Ky Med Assoc*, 85(6):317-322, 1987.

III / RISK FINANCING

Editor's Note

Risk financing (insurance) has become a necessary part of most business endeavors in both the private and public sectors. Conceptually, the desirability of being insured stems from the need to protect a health care provider of surgical services from the risk of financial disaster in the event that injuries should occur to a recipient of those goods or services.

Medical malpractice liability insurance provides those of us in the medical profession with just such a safety net. The changing nature of the practice of medicine today, particularly with regard to the sometimes unrealistic expectations of society, the rapid development of new technology, and the excesses of our legal system, have forced surgeons to become knowledgeable in the area of medical malpractice insurance.

This chapter describes the evolution of the insurance system and the factors the surgeon should consider in selecting coverage. Additional mechanisms through which a surgeon can gain coverage, such as through risk retention groups, joint underwriting associations (JUAs), and patient compensation funds (PCFs) are also described in detail. The forms of coverage, such as claims-made versus occurrence policies, are also explained. Finally, the special needs of residents with regard to insurance are also discussed.

In the decade from 1975 to 1985, ever-increasing claim costs resulted in dramatic increases in the cost of medical liability insurance. Premiums for most surgeons reached extraordinary levels and became a major portion of a physician's overhead. Although costs have moderated somewhat in the past few years, the possibility of "runaway" verdicts continues to haunt the profession, underscoring the need for careful selection of insurance protection.

The availability of insurance coverage is no longer a problem. In fact, in many states surgeons have a choice of at least two carriers. The purchase of medical liability coverage is not without pitfalls, however, and a physician should have a clear understanding of the options that are available in order to make an informed and intelligent decision.

Differences in cost between the carriers may make the decision appear to be an easy one. But decisions about insurance coverage should never be based on cost alone. The financial security of the insurance company, the policyholder's access to state *guaranty funds* in the event of the company's insolvency, the commitment of the company to medical liability insurance, its philosophy about and disposition to resisting groundless claims, and whether the policy provides assurance that no case will be settled without the physician's consent are equally important considerations.

Insurance Carriers

Physician-owned insurance companies provide more than 60 percent of the coverage required by private practitioners in the United States, covering 177,000 physicians in 40 states. For the most part, these companies were started by state medical societies in 1975 and 1976, when the commercial insurance industry was largely abandoning the medical liability market. Although these companies may differ in organizational form, they all are owned and managed by physicians. With only a few exceptions, they are not in business to make a profit and typically use investment income to reduce premiums and sponsor risk management programs, and emphasize peer review among those they insure.

Among commercial insurance companies that still are in the medical liability market, the St. Paul Insurance Company is the largest in terms of premium volume. Other commercial carriers tend to confine their medical liability business to a few states or, perhaps, to one specialty group.

As a result of the availability crisis of 1975, many states now require property and casualty insurance companies to share the medical liability risk through the formation of Joint Underwriting Associations (JUAs). Over time, as the physician-sponsored companies have increased, these JUAs have come to be regarded primarily as a secondary resource, available to physicians who do not wish to, or cannot, purchase insurance from other carriers. The JUAs do, however, remain the only source of insurance coverage in some states, including Massachusetts and Rhode Island.

So-called channelling programs also exist in several states. These programs provide for the coverage of a physician under the insurance of the hospital he or she is affiliated with and share the limits of coverage with that hospital or perhaps with several hospitals. A physician-owned company may provide coverage for hospitals, and those physicians who have one of those hospitals as their primary affiliation may obtain a premium discount under a joint defense program.

In 1986, federal legislation permitted the formation of *risk retention* or purchasing groups to provide nationwide coverage for affiliated groups. Once licensed in one state, the insurance entity providing this coverage can write insurance in all other states without conforming to the normal regulatory requirements of those states. It should be noted, however, that state guaranty funds will not protect policyholders if such a company becomes insolvent.

Physicians whose claims experience is so adverse that they are unable to obtain coverage within their own state may seek coverage through so-called surplus line companies. However, these companies are not licensed by the state, and their premiums are significantly higher than state-regulated premiums.

Patient compensation funds (PCFs) also have been established in several states. These funds provide coverage for providers over a basic minimum of insurance purchased by physicians and hospitals. To participate in a PCF, insured physicians are required by the state to pay a special contribution in addition to their basic coverage. In Pennsylvania, for example, physicians must buy insurance coverage of $200,000 to $600,000, then pay a percentage of their premium (at this writing, 50 percent) to the fund, which provides an additional $1 million to $3 million in coverage. In Indiana, physicians are insured for $100,000 to $300,000, and the fund provides coverage of up to $750,000, the statutory limit on liability awards.

The Limits of Coverage

In most states, the limits on primary coverage are $1 million for each occurrence and $3 million in the aggregate for all occurrences within the period the policy remains in effect, although insurers in several states offer single limits of $5 million (the limit may go as high as $10 million in a few states). Many hospitals require specified limits of protection as a condition of staff privileges, and this requirement has consistently withstood legal challenge. Hospital medical staffs also now frequently establish requirements for basic levels of coverage independently from their hospitals.

Although the high-risk surgical specialties of neurosurgery, obstetrics/gynecology, and orthopaedic surgery have the greatest exposure to costly settlements, *all* physicians, including those who are not surgeons, run the risk of very large verdicts. Therefore, each physician should determine the limits of coverage he or she requires based on consideration of all relevant circumstances and after careful deliberation and consultation with the physician's insurance broker, carrier, and, perhaps, personal counsel.

Forms of Coverage

In theory, physicians may purchase one of two available forms of insurance coverage: *occurrence* or *claims-made*. Occurrence policies provide coverage for all incidents that occur during the period covered by the policy, no matter when they come to light. Claims-made policies cover only those incidents that occur *and are reported* during the policy period. The initial cost of claims-made coverage is deceptively less expensive than occurrence coverage. In fact, because only about one-third of the incidents that occur in a given year are actually reported in that year, the charge for claims-made coverage in the first year will be only about one-third of the occurrence rate. Subsequently, however, usually in five to six years, claims-made rates rise significantly and eventually equal the occurrence rate. Thus, a mature claims-made policy may cost more than an occurrence policy. In addition, once a claims-made policy is canceled, physicians must have protection for incidents that occurred while the policy was in force, but which do not come to light until after cancellation. This protection is referred to as reporting endorsement coverage, or, more popularly, *tail coverage*. This coverage must be purchased at the time the claims-made policy expires and, in effect, converts a claims-made into an occurrence policy.

Physicians who purchase claims-made policies also need to be aware of policy terms related to the reporting endorsement. Most carriers provide an automatic, or free, reporting endorsement under certain circumstances, such as the death or disability of the policyholder or the retirement of the policyholder from medical practice after having been in the company's claims-made program for a specified number of years or having reached a specified retirement age. Unfortunately, a physician who finds it necessary to cancel a claims-made policy because of a move to another state or a change in the nature of the physician's practice will find the purchase of a reporting endorsement very expensive. For example, a physician in New York in the third year of a claims-made cycle would pay almost one-and-one-half times the present occurrence rate to purchase a reporting endorsement. Physicians considering entering a partnership or employment arrangement should be aware of this risk and clearly establish who will bear the cost of buying a reporting endorsement, should one become necessary.

As a practical matter, however, a physician's options may, in fact, be more limited than this discussion would suggest, inasmuch as many companies now offer only claims-made coverage.

The Special Needs of Residents

Most residents are aware of the dangers of professional liability suits and the effect that threat has had on the practice of their specialty, but residents face other professional liability issues related to malpractice or risk management of which they may not be aware. Although less well recognized, these insurance issues can nonetheless have a significant effect on the resident's future ability to practice medicine.

Most residents assume that professional liability insurance will be provided for them by their residency programs. However, a resident needs to know more than simply whether liability insurance is provided. Other, perhaps more crucial, questions should be asked.

What type of coverage is provided by the program? Will claims arising out of the residency be covered if they are made after the resident leaves the program? As the preceding discussion indicates, occurrence coverage protects the resident for all claims resulting from the period of the policy, regardless of when the claim is made. Thus, a resident covered by an occurrence policy would be protected by all malpractice claims arising from the residency, even if, for example, a claim for an impaired infant arising out of an obstetrics residency were made years after the residency were completed.

In contrast, if the resident is covered by a claims-made policy, the insurance company has no obligation to cover claims made after the policy expires, and the resident is protected after leaving the residency program only if tail coverage has been purchased.

Residency programs throughout the United States are likely to provide either occurrence coverage or claims-made coverage for their residents; seldom do they offer both. Because the residency employment contract may not include information about professional liability insurance, a resident should make every effort to obtain and keep copies of the program's master professional liability insurance policy, as well as a written statement or certificate of the coverage provided.

In addition, recognizing that claims can be made years after a residency is completed and that some residency programs and insurance companies periodically purge their files, residents should obtain evidence of insurance for each year of their residency and retain this evidence in their files indefinitely.

Equally important, those who are covered by a claims-made policy should be sure that tail coverage is provided upon the completion of the residency, lest they find themselves with no coverage for claims made after the residency ends.

How much coverage is provided for the resident by the program is another important matter to determine, inasmuch as the coverage provided by some programs may be limited to a certain amount per incident and a certain aggregate amount. In some states, residents' liability is limited by statute or by treating residents as state employees. Other states have established PCFs that reduce the amount of primary insurance that is needed by a resident. Thus, it is impossible to generalize about what constitutes an inadequate amount of insurance for a resident. The question is further complicated by the fact that residents have little power to negotiate for greater amounts of coverage. Nonetheless, every resident should know the limits of his or her coverage and the requirements and special circumstances of the state in which the residency takes place.

Does the policy place any limitations on practice? Most residency liability policies are subject to certain restrictions or exclusions, and residents should be aware of them, because liability coverage will not be provided for claims resulting from activities that violate them.

The most common of these exclusions is for moonlighting activities—that is, events that may occur while the resident is practicing at a second job in another hospital. In general, the practice of moonlighting is not recommended, and residents should be discouraged from engaging in it for a variety of reasons. For one thing, few residency liability insurance policies provide coverage for these activities; therefore, residents who choose to moonlight would be well advised to investigate whether the second institution provides insurance coverage. If coverage is not provided, the resident must either obtain appropriate coverage personally or run the risk of being uninsured for any claims that could result.

What effect would a claim have on the resident's future ability to obtain liability insurance? Even residents whose coverage ensures that adequate amounts will be available to cover all claims resulting from the residency should be aware of an insurance practice known as surcharging or experience rating. Insurers frequently set higher premium rates on claim experience, either in the form of a surcharge in addition to the basic premium or a higher basic premium. Bowing to consumer demands and the belief that the malpractice crisis has been caused by a small number of so-called bad physicians, some insurance companies and state insurance commissions have applied these rating practices to malpractice insurance.

Because it is not uncommon for a plaintiff's attorney to file suit against all health care providers whose names appear in a plaintiff's medical chart, including all residents, a physician who has experienced a number of malpractice claims during residency should investigate the surcharging or experience rating practices of prospective insurance carriers and states prior to entering private practice. Neglecting to do so may mean finding that malpractice insurance is either unavailable or prohibitively expensive.

An Additional Word of Advice

This treatment of the subject of medical liability insurance must, of necessity, be general in nature and is intended only to make the reader aware of the issues that should be considered in making intelligent decisions. Specific circumstances will, of course, vary from individual to individual and from state to state. Therefore, seeking the advice of the state medical society or local chapter of the American College of Surgeons is strongly recommended to those making choices involving liability insurance.

IV / RISK PREVENTION

Editor's Note

The cornerstone of risk prevention is the surgeon's technical and intellectual competence, which is an important and implied consideration in any discussion of this topic. Another very important factor is the development and maintenance of a good surgeon-patient relationship. This chapter discusses ways in which the surgeon can strengthen this relationship and minimize the possibility of litigation if there is an adverse patient occurrence.

The process of informed consent is explained in detail. Various aids that can be used to ensure that the process is appropriate and that the patient is truly informed are described.

The importance of providing adequate documentation is clearly and concisely outlined. In addition, certain guidelines that must be observed, particularly when an adverse event occurs in caring for a patient, are explained.

In an effort to help surgeons minimize the occurrence of missed communications, specific documentation systems that should be used in either the surgeon's office or in an ambulatory surgery center are outlined in detail.

Next, the role of risk prevention in the department of surgery is described. Because of the strong overlap between risk management and quality assurance, special consideration is given to the evolving requirements of the Joint Commission on Accreditation of Health Care Organizations, and suggestions are made to aid surgeons who are responsible for this function in their hospital departments.

Finally, the special position that the resident occupies in the dynamics of quality assurance and risk management, and his or her role in the department in that regard, are discussed.

Surgeon-Patient Relationship

Patient confidence is essential to a satisfactory patient-surgeon relationship, and that confidence is likely to be directly linked to the patient's belief that the surgeon is competent, caring, compassionate, and concerned about the patient's outcome. No matter how skilled the surgeon, a patient may have a difficult surgical experience or a poor outcome, resulting in an adverse impact on the relationship. Unfortunately, given the existing medical-legal climate, the surgeon therefore is reluctantly forced to view each patient as a potential litigant.

Family members of the patient represent another potential hazard to the patient-surgeon relationship. Lacking assurance that the surgeon is concerned about the patient's outcome, family members can contribute to patient anxiety or suspicion, and the surgeon who is not aware of the importance of family concerns increases the risk of introducing a negative or even adversarial aspect to the relationship.

How, then, can the surgeon nurture the confidence of patients and those who are likely to have a significant impact on their attitudes?

The task is not made easier by the fact that the surgeon does not always enjoy the benefits of an orderly, planned encounter. Indeed, the surgeon's first contact with the patient is as likely to occur in an emergency situation in which the patient is unconscious or otherwise unreceptive as it is in the course of a routine office visit. Whatever the circumstances of the encounter, it is imperative that the surgeon take care to communicate calmness and competence. To the patient or family member who is already experiencing the stress that is likely to be associated with the circumstances that necessitated the encounter, any careless word or gesture could be the one that triggers the erosion of the delicate patient-surgeon relationship. Therefore, every encounter with the patient, no matter how seemingly insignificant, warrants thoughtful assessment of its potential impact on that relationship.

The Office Visit

A patient's first contact with a surgeon frequently is via the receptionist who answers the surgeon's office telephone. The impression the patient receives in that encounter can set the tone for the relationship that is to follow. Politeness is, of course, absolutely essential, as is a tone of voice that engenders confidence. Any hint of impatience, disorganization, or flippancy must be scrupulously avoided.

In scheduling an appointment, the receptionist must be trained and prepared with appropriate questions to determine the patient's problem and realistically estimate the amount of time the patient will require. To facilitate information-gathering during the initial visit, the patient should be instructed to bring to the office all medications that he or she may be taking, as well as any laboratory reports and X rays related to the reason for the visit. The patient also should be asked to arrive 15 minutes prior to the first visit to allow time in which to complete registration forms.

Patients arriving at a surgeon's office for the first time are frequently ill and almost invariably anxious. When a person is in that state of mind, little is more disconcerting than the sight of an office reception area overflowing with waiting patients. Being required to wait beyond the appointed time to see the surgeon is almost certain to aggravate any negative feelings the patient already is grappling with. Therefore, it is essential that, to the greatest degree possible, appointments be kept on schedule.

IV / Risk Prevention

When delays are unavoidable—and every surgeon encounters such delays—every effort should be made to contact patients by telephone prior to their arrival to reschedule their appointments. When that is not possible and a patient has been kept waiting, taking time to *personally apologize* for the patient's inconvenience and explain the reason for the delay can go a long way toward defusing any resentment the patient understandably may feel; doing so will, at the same time, avoid giving the appearance of arrogance that busy surgeons may too often inadvertently convey.

Of course, any patient who arrives with fresh lacerations or injury should be seen without delay, leaving the details of registration and identification to be dealt with after the urgency of the situation has been addressed. Delays in responding to a patient's urgent needs are as bad for good patient relations as they are for good patient care.

Once the consultation begins, the patient expects and should receive the surgeon's undivided attention. Taking steps to ensure that telephone calls and other potential sources of interruption are not allowed to interfere with the process is one tangible way to demonstrate the surgeon's genuine concern about the patient.

Beginning the consultation with a detailed history-taking can enhance that demonstration of concern. Any medical problem the patient has encountered, past or present, is important to that patient, and failing to provide an opportunity to talk about it can leave the patient with the impression that the surgeon is unconcerned or the consultation incomplete. This discussion also affords the surgeon the opportunity to communicate to the patient, both through vocal intonation and body language, the attitude of concerned, reasoned, friendly, and professional interest that the surgeon should seek to convey. It is very important that the surgeon have good listening skills. As an initial step in the information-gathering process, the history-taking can also provide a logical introduction to the physical evaluation, thereby easing the transition to what can be a stressful experience for the patient.

Once the history-taking and physical examination have been completed, it is time for the surgeon to make treatment recommendations, recommendations that often will involve an operation. First, however, the patient must be advised of all the options that are available, including the option of relying on observation only. The surgeon's goal at this point should be to promote discussion of the available options with the patient rather than to dictate a decision or press for one point of view.

Indeed, any indication of confusion or uncertainty on the part of the patient or family member should be a signal to the surgeon to proceed cautiously in asking for a decision. The importance of obtaining informed consent for any surgical procedure cannot be emphasized enough. The issue of whether or not consent was truly informed may subsequently be open to challenge if any question arises that the consenting party was under duress to make a decision.

Preparing Patients for an Operation

Helping the patient who elects to undergo a surgical procedure understand and deal with the implications of that decision affords the surgeon another opportunity to communicate caring and concern. Having an operation is likely to be a frightening prospect for many patients. Helping them understand and deal with their apprehensions is an excellent way to establish trust between patient and surgeon, creating a climate of understanding and cooperation rather than one of fear and resistance.

The surgeon also can make an important contribution toward helping the patient prepare for hospitalization. Because many patients are reluctant to confess ignorance of hospital procedures, the surgeon must assume responsibility for describing each event that is likely to occur, including the admitting process, laboratory tests, and the preoperative visits of nurses, anesthesiologists, or other consultants, as well as for discussing such matters as what medications the patient may be given and why they are required. No other source of information, no matter how informative and valuable, is likely to be as reassuring to the patient as a personal explanation by the surgeon. Similarly, while skilled assistants may provide information to patients that reinforces the information they receive from the surgeon, assistants should be viewed as supplements in the information process and never as substitutes for the surgeon.

Asking the patient to designate a spouse, parent, or other person to communicate with the surgeon on his or her behalf in the immediate postoperative period is another way to provide support to the patient while strengthening the patient-surgeon relationship. The presence of loved ones often is seen as crucial to the patient's comfort and successful recovery. The experience is likely to be a far more positive one for all if family members or concerned friends are briefed on such matters as when the patient will be taken to the surgical suite, how long the operation is likely to take, and where the surgeon will meet with them after completing the operation. Providing a detailed discussion of the outcome of the procedure as soon as it is completed in language that a layperson can understand is, of course, essential to nurturing trust.

The Postoperative Period

The period following the operation affords additional opportunities in this regard. With third-party payors now often mandating the number of days a patient can be hospitalized, many surgical patients are discharged sooner than in previous times. In addition, some procedures that once would have been performed while the patient was hospitalized are now performed on an outpatient basis. Thus, it is not uncommon for a patient to experience some event at home after an operation that nursing care might have resolved if the patient were hospitalized. In that event, patients are likely to seek the surgeon's advice. The frustration a patient can experience by having to deal with an impersonal answering service can quickly turn to anger, and that anger can undermine whatever rapport existed between surgeon and patient. Thus, simply remaining available throughout the postoperative period to answer questions and provide assurance may be as important to a positive outcome as postoperative care itself.

Postoperatively, a pattern of consistency should be established. The surgeon represents the patient's security—an anchor at a time of pain and suffering. The patient should be better acquainted with his or her surgeon than with those on the surgical floor who care for the patient. Postoperative rounds should be made regularly, and, if possible, rounds should not be delegated to others. The patient has hired the surgeon. If all goes well, the patient may simply wonder at the surgeon's decreased attention once the surgical procedure has been completed, but any adverse event may lead the patient to ask if the complication could have been avoided if the physician had been more attentive after the operation.

The patient or the patient's family should not be abandoned when the outcome is poor. It is even more important at these times to foster compassionate communication between physician and patient.[1] The surgeon should be available to address a patient's problem and plans for treatment.

Surgeon's Rights

The surgeon, while addressing the rights of the patient, is also entitled to certain rights, such as the right to restrict the scope of specialty practice. If required treatment is beyond this specialty, the surgeon has the obligation to refer the patient to an appropriate specialist. The surgeon also has the right to limit practice to a certain geographic area or community; to be unavailable, provided that a competent substitute has been designated; to determine the time and frequency of appointments; to refuse to make house calls; and to refuse a request for what may be considered a less appropriate method of treatment.

Consent and the Process of Informed Consent

Informed consent is a consent obtained after adequate disclosure.[2] What adequate disclosure is differs throughout the United States. Because obtaining consent is so important, every surgeon, with the help of the state medical society, ACS chapters, or private counsel, should identify the consent requirements that apply in the state in which the surgeon practices and take steps to ensure that the surgeon's practice complies with those requirements. However, it is almost universally agreed that the patient should be given the pertinent information about the proposed treatment in each of the following categories: (1) the diagnosis, (2) the nature and purpose of the proposed treatment, (3) the prognosis if the proposed treatment is carried out, (4) the risks associated with the proposed treatment, (5) the feasible treatment alternatives (as well as the likelihood of success and the risks associated with each), and (6) the prognosis if the treatment is refused.

The process of obtaining informed consent should not just be viewed as a signing of a consent sheet. Ideally, the process of consent starts when the patient and surgeon first meet to discuss a problem. The surgeon-patient relationship stressed in the previous chapter is important. Consent is a continuing education process that results in a joint decision to pursue a specific treatment plan. Both participants—the surgeon and the patient—are on the same team battling the same enemy: disease or disability. Both hope for the best result, but neither has unrealistic expectations. The signing of the consent form is merely a formality, signifying that the goal of full disclosure has been accomplished.

Some physicians mistakenly believe that the process of informed consent is necessary only for surgical and other invasive procedures. In fact, informed consent is required for all treatment, whether therapeutic or diagnostic, invasive or noninvasive, surgical or medical. Therefore, whatever the recommended treatment, a frank discussion between surgeon and patient about treatment alternatives may be necessary, even in the event that no treatment is recommended.

Failure to obtain a patient's informed consent is legally excused in only three instances.

First, obtaining informed consent is excused when a legitimate medical emergency necessitates immediate treatment, but the patient is unable to give consent and no one who is authorized to consent on behalf of the patient is readily available. In such an event, the surgeon should document the nature of the emergency and the need for immediate treatment, obtain a consultation to confirm that a medical emergency exists, note the reasons why the patient could not give consent, and record the efforts made to locate and obtain the consent from the patient's next of kin.

Second, informed consent is also legally excused when therapeutic privilege to withhold information is applicable. However, surgeons would be well advised not to rely on therapeutic privilege because the courts have been reluctant to apply it. Therefore, the surgeon who is absolutely convinced that frank disclosure would interfere with treatment, must take extreme care to document the reasons for that opinion, obtain a consulting opinion confirming the reasonableness of the conclusion, and communicate with the patient's next of kin. In making disclosure to the next of kin, surgeons should carefully consider the patient's rights to confidentiality and privacy.

Third, some patients do not want to be informed about such matters as the risks and complications of a surgical procedure or its prognosis. In that event, it is essential to obtain the patient's signature on a written statement of that fact.

To meet informed consent requirements, discussion of the risks and benefits and alternatives to a treatment must take place before the treatment is rendered. More importantly, the discussion must take place before the patient signs a consent form. By signing the consent form, the patient acknowledges that the necessary information has been conveyed and, where required by state law, that the patient has had adequate opportunity to ask questions and have them answered in a satisfactory manner.

For a number of reasons, the surgeon's office is the ideal setting in which to hold a discussion of and obtain consent for surgical operation. First, obtaining consent and initiating treatment at two different times is more likely to enable the patient to adequately consider his or her decision, thus reducing the risk that a question subsequently may arise regarding whether the patient was pressured to proceed with treatment or given insufficient time in which to consider relevant information. In addition, the surgeon retains greater control over the circumstances in which the consent is obtained and therefore should be better able to implement protocols to ensure adequate disclosure and documentation of the process.

Obtaining consent in the surgeon's office also reduces the likelihood that a patient can claim that the surgeon was unavailable to discuss the treatment and answer questions, or that the consent form was signed while the patient was under the influence of medication, as is more likely in the hospital setting, and was not cognizant of what was being signed. Nor is the patient likely to be able to claim, as some have, that the consent form was just another of the many forms he or she was asked to sign on admission to the hospital and that the patient therefore had not realized what was being signed. The presence of a nurse in the room at the time of a surgeon's discussion with the patient offers additional confirmation. In the office setting, the nurse can be asked to sign the consent form as a witness of the circumstances under which it was obtained.

Any surgeon who has performed a procedure hundreds of times is likely to have difficulty recalling exactly what one particular patient was told. Thus, if the surgeon's recollection were challenged, it would be extremely difficult to provide assurances that the surgeon could accurately recall in detail a conversation that might have taken place years in the past. In the event of a lawsuit, therefore, a surgeon will be able to testify only as to what is customarily told such a patient, while the patient who has undergone a surgical procedure only once may be believed to be able to recall the conversation in detail. For these reasons, it would be wise for the surgeon to make a note of the explanation given to the patient, particularly that portion related to the general nature of the risks involved.

Many patients prefer to include family members in a discussion of planned treatment, and therefore, it is recommended that one or more family members be present at this time, with the patient's permission. If, for some reason (for example, in the case of a very old or infirm patient), the surgeon believes it necessary, the family may also be conferred with in the absence of the patient. These conversations would, of course, be duly noted in the medical record. Due consideration, however, should be given to the patient's prior expression of a desire for confidentiality. Remember, also, that it is the decision of the competent patient, and not that of the family, that is paramount.

Because only the surgeon has sufficient information on the patient's background, the expertise needed to evaluate risks, the ability to answer patients' questions, and knowledge of why one form of treatment has been recommended over others, the courts have concluded that the surgeon is responsible for obtaining a patient's informed consent, rather than the hospital or its nurses. In most states, therefore, it is the surgeon's ultimate responsibility to provide patients with sufficient information to permit them to give an informed consent. A physician who merely includes an order to get a consent form signed, together with other preoperative orders, would have a difficult time successfully mounting a defense against such a claim if the information conveyed by the nurse was inaccurate or inadequate.

The Joint Commission on Accreditation of Healthcare Organizations (JCAHO) requires the hospital record to contain evidence that the patient's consent to treatment was obtained. Most hospital attorneys advise nurses to refer patients' questions to their surgeon and to discourage an uninformed patient from signing the hospital's consent form. In the interest of their own protection, nurses also are advised to record patients' requests for information about scheduled treatment and referrals for such information to the patient's physician.

The Consent Form

In most states, verbal consent to treatment is valid. However, this form of consent makes it difficult to prove exactly what was said, thereby placing the surgeon at a disadvantage in the event of a subsequent lawsuit. The physician would suffer the same disadvantage if verbal consent were documented only by an entry in progress notes or office records. The more prudent course is to follow the process of informed consent, which includes, but is not limited to, documenting a patient's consent on a form that details the information disclosed to the patient and to have it signed by both patient and surgeon and witnessed by a hospital or office nurse.

To protect against liability for lack of informed consent, each surgeon's office should develop a series of standard consent forms for each procedure that is regularly performed by the surgeon. Although some physicians rely on a single generalized consent form indicating the patient's consent for "medical treatment" and stating that "the risks of the procedure have been explained" to the patient, such a form would be of little value in proving the exact nature of the disclosures made to the patient. A consent form that is specifically tailored to the procedure to be performed conclusively establishes exactly what disclosures were made, and thus can be a significant deterrent to an informed consent claim.

Any surgeon who doubts the value of developing consent forms detailing the specific risks of the procedure to be performed would do well to consider the size of the judgment that might be awarded in the event that a complication of surgical operation arose, and a jury concluded that the risk of the complication should have been disclosed. In fact, as a general rule, the more elective the procedure and the greater the number of therapeutic alternatives, the more detailed the disclosure should be; every consent form should disclose the risks of death, brain damage, and paralysis to a patient who is to undergo general anesthesia.

Using a consent form that has been drafted by an attorney and endorsed by the state medical society and that conforms to other consent forms in use throughout the state should be advantageous to the surgeon in the event of litigation. Each state, through its courts or legislature, has developed its own informed consent doctrine. For that reason, although a court in one state may have concluded that a certain risk need not be disclosed, that fact is no guarantee that a court in another state will reach the same conclusion. Many states do not dictate exactly what is required in a consent form.

Still, however, there are certain general principles to keep in mind in drafting a consent form, among them:

1. Use medical terminology supplemented with a clear explanation of each medical term in language a layperson can be expected to understand.

2. All commonly occurring risks of the procedure should be listed, including those associated with anesthesia. When possible, the anesthesiologist should personally advise the patient of anesthesia risks. If it is unclear whether

IV / Risk Prevention

or not a particular risk should be included, it is wise to err on the side of disclosure.

3. A risk should never be minimized by describing it in the consent form as something that is extraordinarily rare or unlikely to occur. The words "simple," "uncomplicated," or "minor" should never be used to describe a procedure, and every consent form should include a statement that no result has been guaranteed.

4. With rare exceptions, the use of statistics should be avoided inasmuch as it may be argued that national statistics may be misleading if the physician's own experience varies from the norm.

5. The fact that a patient has been given an informational brochure or shown an audiovisual aid should be noted on the consent form.

6. The patient should be asked to acknowledge in writing that the information disclosed has been understood, that an opportunity to ask questions has been provided, and that all questions have been answered to the patient's satisfaction.

7. Ideally, the signatures of both patient and surgeon should be required on the consent form to establish that both were present for the discussion, and the time and date on which the discussion occurred should be indicated.

8. Each consent form should conclude with an omnibus consent provision, such as the following, from the ACS *Patient Safety Manual*[3]:

    4. Complications; Unforeseen Conditions; Results
    I am aware that in the practice of medicine, other unexpected risks or complications not discussed may occur. I also understand that during the course of the proposed procedure(s) unforeseen conditions may be revealed requiring the performance of additional procedures, and I authorize such procedures to be performed. I further acknowledge that no guarantees or promises have been made to me concerning the results of any procedure or treatment.

It should be noted that such a provision may be legally worthless and must never be used as a substitute for discussing foreseeable contingencies and noting them in the consent form. However, its inclusion in the consent form may serve as a deterrent to legal action.

Practical Approaches to Disclosure

As a practical matter, of course, the informed consent doctrine poses a practice management challenge, seeming to demand more time for discussion with each patient than the busy physician's time might permit. One possible solution in the case of patients who are seen in the physician's office prior to having an operation is to establish a protocol for disclosure that enlists the assistance of office staff members.

Essential information on the proposed procedure, the therapeutic alternatives, and their risks can be conveyed to the patient through the use of informational aids such as a well-designed brochure or videotape. Pamphlets, videos, and other forms of informational aids are, of course, commercially available for this purpose. However, in-house production of information tools allows for easy and economical updating. The aid need not be elaborately or expensively prepared—printed material can be no more complicated than a stapled set of typewritten pages, while a videotape may simply show the physician at his or her desk talking to the camera as though he or she were talking to a patient.

Once such aids are available in the office, a patient who is to undergo a procedure can be referred to a member of the office staff, who can provide written materials to the patient or schedule a viewing of audiovisual material. Next, you might want to give the patient the consent form to read and then provide an opportunity for the patient to raise any questions about the procedure. When the information-giving process has been completed and the consent form signed by the patient, the title of the information aid used should be noted on the consent form, together with the name of the office employee who can attest to the fact that these steps were taken. It is also recommended that each time an informational piece is updated, copies of earlier versions be maintained on file so that they can be used to document exactly what information was conveyed to a given patient. It must be stressed, however, that the dialogue between the patient and the surgeon is mandatory, regardless of the informational aids.

Developing informational aids does require an initial investment of time and effort, but that investment is likely to be very quickly recouped in the form of more efficient use of the physician's time. At the same time, it is likely that their use will help keep patients both better and more consistently informed.

Obtaining Consent in Special Circumstances

Obtaining appropriate consent may be a more complicated process when the patient is a minor, mentally ill or deficient, sedated, in shock, or in great pain. Requirements vary from state to state, but it is likely that such circumstances will require that disclosures be made to and consent obtained from the patient's parent or legal guardian, or that the patient's own consent be supplemented by that of another person authorized by law to give consent.

Other circumstances that require special treatment include the need to obtain consent for transplants, sterilization, abortion, experimental therapy, and the removal or withholding of life-support systems. In such special cases, it is strongly recommended that the surgeon obtain legal counsel that is directly relevant to the matter at hand from a qualified attorney.

Finally, the surgeon should be aware that each case brought to litigation is decided on its particular facts and in accordance with the perceived credibility of the various witnesses who testify. For those reasons, unless the highest appellate court of a state determines—as a matter of law, rather than on the evidence presented at the trial—that a particular risk need not be disclosed, courts (even those in the same state) may arrive at conflicting decisions.

Proper Documentation—
The Medical Record

Medical records, both hospital and office charts, are extremely important in the management of risk. In addition to documenting the care given to a patient, they serve as the vehicle for communicating data needed by all members of the patient's health care team, charting the course of care rendered in the hospital and outlining plans for the patient's present and future care.[1]

Medical records also have legal status. As such, they are a fiduciary responsibility and may become a legal document for later review. Required by the government, they also must satisfy requirements outlined by the Joint Commission on Accreditation of Healthcare Organizations and in hospital bylaws.

What is not written in the medical record is legally presumed not to have occurred. In fact, to paraphrase R. S. Brittain, writing about medical-legal cases in *The Practicing Surgeon's Perspective*: "Reality is not what happened or what you say happened; reality is what is in the medical record."[4]

The medical record is invaluable as a patient care tool. When carefully and meticulously kept, it also can be an indelible line of defense in these litigious times. As D. Danner has written in *Medical Malpractice: A Primer for Physicians*, "In the courtroom, medical records are witnesses whose memory never dies."[1]

But care must be taken to ensure that medical records will meet the rigorous tests to which they would be put if presented in the courtroom. Toward that end, the surgeon should approach recordkeeping with certain suggestions in mind.

- **All entries should be neat, legible, and written in ink**

  A well-kept chart enables the health care provider to reconstruct the patient's course of treatment and demonstrate that the care provided to a patient was in accordance with accepted medical practice.[1] Therefore, a physician must always maintain complete and adequate records, including records of important negative events.

- **Each entry should be signed with the physician's first and last names and professional designation**

- **Each entry should note the date and time it was made**

  Entries should be made in a timely fashion and in chronological order.

- **Each page of the record should be dated and labeled with the patient's name**

- **Inappropriate skipping of lines or spaces should be avoided**

  If a blank space remains at the end of an entry, a line should be drawn through it.

- **Only standard abbreviations and symbols should be used, and ditto marks and initials should be avoided**

  Records should be written in accepted medical terminology, and abbreviations should be avoided.

- **Supplemental pages may be used, if necessary, to record missed notes, which should be indicated as late entries**

- **Medical records should be restricted to statements of fact**

  All entries to the medical record should be pertinent, relevant, and objective.[5] The recording of impressions or tentative diagnoses should be avoided; however, if they must be recorded, they should be clearly labeled as such. Opinions and descriptions of treatment plans should be backed by statements of relevant facts, and explanations should be given for choices and decisions made. For example, if certain diseases have been ruled out, that fact should be recorded to indicate to anyone who may

IV / Risk Prevention

later review the chart that treatment alternatives were considered in the course of determining the plan that was followed.

- **Medical records should never be erased**

    Medical records must never be altered. If any corrections or additions must be made, they should be added to the chart in regular sequence, with appropriate reference to the previous entries. This procedure is strongly recommended because changes in records, such as notes added and comments entered out of order, can easily be detected. Where corrections must be made, one line should be used to cancel incorrect entries and the time and date of the cancellation noted, together with the initials of the person making the change. Appropriate corrections should be entered chronologically, and care must be taken to avoid giving the appearance that the records have been tampered with.[1] Altered records, if at issue, are easily detected by experts and can substantially weaken a physician's defense in court in the event of a dispute.[5]

The following items should all be documented in the medical record.

- **All missed appointments and other indicators of possible lack of patient compliance**

    Any problems that develop in the course of a patient's care must be addressed in the medical record. These notes should be consistently recorded, not only in their statements of facts but also in writing style. In other words, the notes should never be suddenly expanded upon or take on a defensive tone.

- **The dates of all referrals and return visits**

    If the physician has any questions about the care of the patient, he or she should be sure to obtain appropriate consultations. Those consulting opinions, which can be extremely valuable if questions later arise about the conduct of patient care, should be duly recorded.[4]

- **Content of all telephone calls**

    The time and content of all telephone calls should be noted. Telephone conversations conducted after the surgeon's regular office hours should be documented immediately after their completion. Details of the conversation should be subsequently entered into the office chart and initialed. Surgeons who take telephone calls for another surgeon should provide details or summaries of them that can be transmitted to the office of the patient's regular surgeon.

- **All prescriptions written and refills needed**

    The name of the drug, the dosage, the directions for taking the medication, and the number of pills or tablets should be recorded, as well as the number of refills.

- **Verbal follow-up care instructions**

    Instructions given to the patient must be recorded in the chart and signed.

- **Distribution of educational and informational materials to patients**

    Medical records should be as complete as possible. All instructions or informational materials given to the patient should be identified in the record.

- **Poor clinical outcomes and treatment plans for complications**

- **Explanations for any instances in which the notes made by the physician and those entered by the nurse do not agree**

    Care should be taken not to eliminate the nurse's notes; rather, the physician should write a follow-up note in appropriate chronological order, making reference to the discrepancy and explaining it.[1]

What should *not* be recorded in the medical record are any personal and disparaging remarks or statements that imply cause and effect. There is no place in the medical record for comments that blame procedures performed by personnel for a particular series of events.

Office and Outpatient Settings

As the employer of many people who are responsible for communicating directly with patients, the surgeon typically is better able to reduce risk in his or her own office and ambulatory care setting than anywhere else. By establishing procedures and expectations and ensuring that office personnel receive appropriate training, the surgeon has far more control over three areas that are crucial in this regard: office procedures, patient rapport, and medical records. Following is a check list of those areas in which special attention should be paid to ensure that all interactions between medical personnel and patients are conducted in a manner that enhances rather than detracts from a good physician-patient relationship.

Office Procedures

Telephone Etiquette

First, of course, it is essential that office staff be aware of the need to be courteous and helpful at all times in dealing with patients, both in person and over the telephone.

Prescription Renewal

Every surgeon's office should have established prescription renewal procedures. In those offices where the physician delegates permission to office personnel to renew prescriptions, the procedures should specify that prescriptions may be renewed only with the physician's verbal approval and that the physician's approval must be documented in a note signed by the physician in the patient's records.

Housekeeping

Medication and telephone logs should be maintained in both the physician's office and home. These notes should be transcribed in a timely fashion into the patient's chart, and then initialed by the physician. All laboratory and X-ray reports should be initialed and dated by the surgeon before they are filed. Written instructions for drug calculation and administration must be maintained, and care must be taken to ensure that drugs are measured with absolute accuracy and that appropriate methods of administration are adhered to.

Staff Training

In-service training sessions for office and ambulatory care staff should be carried out on a regular basis.

Waste Disposal

Detailed procedures for disposal of infectious waste materials, such as contaminated dressings and used needles, must be written and carefully followed in the office and ambulatory care facility to avoid contamination of patients, office personnel, and those who deal with waste products after their removal from the care setting.

Emergency and Disaster Plans

Mock code blue emergency and disaster plans should be written and kept accessible to staff members to facilitate their implementation during emergencies.

Missed Appointments

Missed appointments should be documented in the patient chart. Patients who miss appointments should be contacted by telephone to learn the reason for their absence and to reschedule the appointment, if appropriate. Following up such telephone calls with a letter can be helpful in reducing the risk of litigation.

Inquiries

All inquiries from attorneys and third parties, subpoenas, depositions, and other materials related to lawsuits should be managed by the physician rather than by members of the office staff.

Billing

The physician should be notified of a delinquent account before any collection action is instituted, because the physician alone may be aware of a circumstance, such as patient dissatisfaction with a treatment outcome, that would argue against pressing for payment.

Incident Reporting

Any incidents involving patient and office staff or physician, or conversations overheard by office personnel that would indicate patient dissatisfaction with care, should be documented and brought to the attention of the physician. The physician should initial the report, which then should be filed in the patient's record.

Patient Termination

Patients may be terminated from a surgeon's practice if the surgeon believes that he or she can no longer care for the patient. The patient also has the right to terminate the relationship. Patients whose nonemergency treatment is to be terminated by the surgeon should be notified by certified mail (1) that the physician is no longer willing to continue treating the patient and (2) that a reasonable amount of time will be allocated to permit the patient to locate a new physician before care is terminated by the surgeon. This procedure should only apply to patients terminated from the practice by the physician, not to patients who are no longer in need of the surgeon's care.

Follow-up Plans

Follow-up plans for each patient should be documented in the office records both in the interest of good patient care and to forestall the possibility of subsequent claims that patients were never instructed to return for follow-up care.

Quality Assurance Activity

The staff of every surgeon's office and ambulatory care setting should perform a self-assessment exercise, or office operations review, twice a year with the use of checklists.

Patient Evaluation

Although optional, an annual evaluation of patients' attitudes toward the surgeon's office and ambulatory setting can be a very helpful tool in avoiding lawsuits.

Patient Rapport

Positive Test Result Notification

Written reports of X-ray examinations or test results that indicate abnormality must be shown to the surgeon and initialed before insertion into the patient's records, and the patient should be promptly notified by the surgeon of the test results. Failure to take these steps could result in an indefensible delay in diagnosis and treatment.

Communication

The importance to a surgeon of constantly striving to improve communications skills cannot be emphasized strongly enough. The surgeon must take time to listen carefully to each patient. Patients must be made to feel that the information being elicited is helpful and necessary to the surgeon in making a diagnosis. Surveys show that the length of time a surgeon spends with a patient is a key factor in patient satisfaction, second in importance only to the amount of information the surgeon provides. Interpreters should be available to assist any patients who do not speak the same language as the physician.

Medical Records

The most common sources of problems in patient records maintained in the surgeon's office or ambulatory care facility are the omission of key words and decimal points, the use of inaccurate words, illegible writing, alterations, and abbreviations. All of these common sources of problems are preventable, provided that certain basic principles are adhered to in the maintenance of medical records. (See the section of this chapter entitled "Proper Documentation—The Medical Record" for a complete discussion.)

Informed Consent Process

This subject is discussed in detail in the section of this chapter entitled "Consent and the Process of Informed Consent."

Departments of Surgery

The increasing number of lawsuits and spiraling amount of monetary settlements of the past 20 years have encouraged hospitals in the United States to develop strong risk management programs, one purpose of which is to reduce preventable adverse patient occurrences that may lead to liability claims. This function of risk management is known as risk prevention. Loss control, another function of risk management, deals with liability after an adverse occurrence, lawsuit, and recognition of liability. Risk prevention evaluates adverse patient occurrences individually and collectively in the interest of avoiding or reducing the incidence of reappearing occurrences.

Risk management and quality assurance programs both are designed to ensure the appropriateness of and to enhance patient care and, as such, have several overlapping functions. For example, both often rely on the same data sources and have similar review processes to assess data for corrective actions.

Despite their similarities, however, risk management and quality assurance programs also differ. Whereas risk management activities seek to reduce liability actions, the goal of quality assurance is to enhance patient care. Another difference is that risk prevention relies heavily on incident reporting, patient complaints, and occurrence reporting, whereas quality assurance uses these data to identify not only trends or patterns but also problems, doing so by monitoring preestablished indicators of appropriate patient care. Both functions rely on committees to assess data, recommend action, and monitor results, but these committees may vary in composition, with risk management committees consisting primarily of administrators, paralegals, and lawyers, and quality assurance committees consisting of physicians and health care professionals. Finally, risk management is often thought of as a hospital function, and quality assurance as a departmental function. In reality, however, the functions and goals of the two programs are very similar, and their activities and objectives are integrated at both levels. This is especially true in relation to the department of surgery, where a large share of liability claims originate as a result of the procedure-oriented nature of surgical practice.

Quality Assurance—A Workable Plan

Quality assurance can help in effective risk prevention. The Joint Commission on Accreditation of Healthcare Organizations (JCAHO) describes the quality assurance function as "an ongoing quality assurance program designed to objectively and systematically monitor and evaluate the quality and appropriateness of patient care, pursue opportunities to improve patient care, and resolve identified problems."[6]

According to the JCAHO, the 10 steps that constitute the quality assurance program are (1) assign responsibility, (2) delineate the scope of care, (3) identify important aspects of care, (4) identify indicators that relate to those aspects of care, (5) establish thresholds for evaluation related to the indicators, (6) collect and organize data, (7) evaluate care when thresholds are reached, (8) take action to improve care, (9) assess the effectiveness of the actions taken and documentation improvement, and (10) communicate relevant information to the organizationwide quality assurance program (see figure on page 137).[7] This 10-step monitoring and evaluation process provides an excellent guide to creating a workable and understandable quality assurance plan. A good quality assurance program

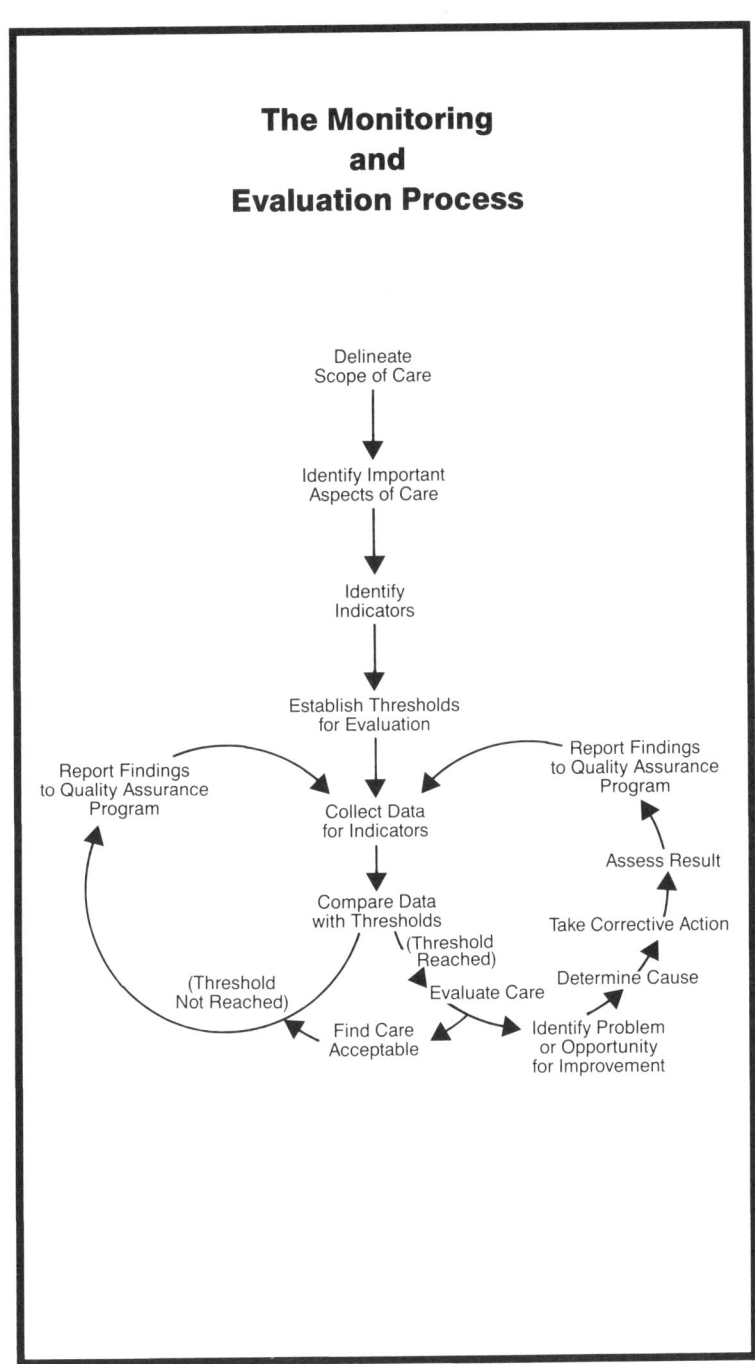

Reprinted with permission of the JCAHO.[7]

consists of five components: purpose, plan, person, participants, and product. The *purpose* of a quality assurance program is to ensure the adequacy and appropriateness of patient care.

Development of a *written plan* provides focus and direction to the quality assurance process, and it is the first step in developing a viable program. The actions that will be taken to achieve improvements and confirm findings will depend on the deficiencies noted. The plan should identify personnel who will be responsible for the various phases of its implementation, the indicators that are to be studied and when they are to be observed for study, by whom data are to be collected, and how and by whom data are to be evaluated.

One individual in each department should be assigned responsibility for coordinating and supervising that department's quality assurance activities. Ideally, this quality assurance coordinator should be a surgeon who can understand the issues that may be raised, relate to other surgeons in the department, and serve as a resource in the development of indicators and data collection. The departmental quality assurance coordinator is responsible for ensuring the development of the indicators and thresholds to be monitored and for overseeing data collection.

In a small department, the responsibility may fall to the chairman or another surgeon who volunteers to undertake the task or be rotated among various surgeons in the department. In a larger, more complex, department that consists of various divisions and special units, learning the job and coordinating its activities are likely to be more demanding and time-consuming. These larger hospital departments require that an individual, usually a surgeon, devote a significant amount of time integrating the quality assurance activities of the various specialty divisions of the department.

Quality assurance programs also require *other participants* to collect and evaluate the data and determine ways in which to improve or correct problems that are identified. Initial data usually are collected by nonphysician personnel, such as nurses, clerks, medical records personnel, and others in the department.

The specific data that will be required must be carefully determined before data collection begins in order to provide nonphysician personnel with the guidelines they will need to accomplish their task. These guidelines often can be furnished by monitoring or surveillance committees or determined based on other sources in the hospital.

In a large hospital, a computerized data bank is desirable to facilitate the organization of reports in a variety of ways, such as by type of complication, location, surgeon, causative factor, and effect on outcome. Data collected in this way next must be submitted for surgeons' review to determine if corrective action is necessary, perhaps as part of the regular monthly departmental meeting.

All primary deliverers of health care—surgeons, nurses, and ancillary personnel—should participate in the development of the indicators and thresholds and should evaluate the data. In that way, all participants in the provision of care can contribute to the quality assurance effort in order to achieve maximum effectiveness.

The *product* of quality assurance is a combination of the identification of problems, based on careful evaluation of the data, together with the corrective actions that are taken and the follow-up assessment that must be done in order to ensure that any corrective actions that are implemented have achieved their objective. A good program also provides for early reporting of adverse occurrences while facts are still fresh and the parties involved easily accessible—an especially important consideration in a teaching institution, where the house staff turnover rate is likely to be high. Early reporting also is more likely to mean early implementation of corrective action and allocation of appropriate funding to accomplish that goal.

The *product* of quality assurance also should include a mechanism for communicating information throughout the department and the institution, when appropriate, as well as good documentation for JCAHO accreditation purposes. This information will aid in the monitoring of practice profiles of each member of the department, which, in turn, may be used in making decisions concerning reappointment or changes in privileges.

Identifying Quality Assurance Issues

One of the most difficult aspects of establishing a quality assurance program is determining what to study. The first step is to delineate the services provided by the department in which the program is to operate and to determine what kinds of conditions and diagnoses are treated. High-volume, high-risk, and problem-prone areas should receive the highest priority. The focus should be on quality of care issues and should be more concerned with the outcome of care rather than with the process of care.

In the context of quality assurance, the term *indicator* is a measure of some aspect of care and should not be confused with an *indication* for surgery. Such an indicator may measure a structure (for example, a kind of equipment), a process (including assessment, treatment, and patient management), or an outcome (complications or short- or long-term results). Some examples of indicators that are easily established are (a) unexpected return to the operating room within the first 24 hours after operation, (b) unscheduled admissions to the hospital after ambulatory surgery, (c) unplanned readmissions to hospital within 30 days of operation, (d) wound infection in clean surgical cases, and (e) appendices that are removed after preoperative diagnoses of acute appendicitis and that, on pathologic examination, are determined to be normal.

Establishing appropriate thresholds is crucial to achieving maximum surgeon involvement while minimizing the time that has to be committed to data review. The threshold for evaluation, by definition, is a preestablished level of performance related to an indicator at which further evaluation of the quality and the appropriateness of an important aspect of care is indicated. Essentially, this is the triggering mechanism when previously defined thresholds for indicators are observed. Threshold-setting can be established based on (1) sentinel event (such as described previously in examples *a*, *b*, and *c*), with a level of 0 percent to 100 percent; (2) guidelines published in the literature (such as seen in example *d*) above 2 percent; or (3) experience in the institution (as seen in example *e*) above 10 percent.

Once the indicator and threshold have been established, appropriate data are collected and screened to determine if the threshold has been exceeded. If the threshold has not been exceeded, no further action is required; if, however, the threshold has been surpassed, the department's surgeons must undertake an in-depth review to determine what is causing the problem and how it can be corrected. Correcting a problem or improving a situation may require such actions as changing a policy, improving communications, reallocating resources, or modifying behavior. Whatever action is indicated, the quality assurance process is not complete until a follow-up evaluation confirms that the situation has improved or the problem resolved. If improvement or resolution has not occurred, and the problem continues, additional corrective action must be developed and documented.

Throughout the process, effective communication of information regarding the evaluation, actions taken, and follow-up activities are essential to the total involvement of all of the participants. Quality assurance information from hospital committees should be distributed to the department at regular intervals, and in large departments, the coordinator should facilitate interdepartmental communication of quality assurance activities, usually through a committee representative of each division.

The Resident

During the past several years, much has been written regarding professional liability and its effects on physicians, other medical care providers, third-party payors, health care recipients, government health programs and their creators, and legislative bodies. Although significant attention has been directed to physicians in general, little heed has been paid to residents or fellows in training.[8] In fact, the only single source of professional liability information that is devoted exclusively to residents has been compiled by members of the Department of Professional Liability of the American College of Obstetricians and Gynecologists (ACOG).[9] That source, with the permission of ACOG, serves as the basis for this discussion.

Accountability and Liability

The climate created by the current level of concern about professional liability has influenced how residents are taught, what they are taught, the breadth of experience that is available to them, the amount of responsibility they are allowed, and who teaches them.

All residents practice as trainees under the supervision of others, whether or not they are licensed. They are supervised by attending staff, clinical faculty, more senior residents, residency program directors, and the staff of the hospital or other institution at which the training occurs. Although those who supervise resident trainees are usually held accountable for their acts, the residents themselves also may be held responsible for their own actions.

PROFESSIONAL LIABILITY/RISK MANAGEMENT – A MANUAL FOR SURGEONS

Failure of a resident or a resident's supervisor to inform a patient of the resident's status may result in causes of action for fraud, deceit, misrepresentation, assault and battery, and lack of informed consent. Patient acceptance or refusal of medical service from the resident also should be documented.

The major source of liability for the resident is failure to meet appropriate standards of care. Residents must never forget that they may not be fully trained to provide all procedures and treatments and therefore should perform only those for which they have been fully trained.

Both the supervising physician and the resident are responsible for providing high-quality care to a patient.* Therefore, it is essential that they establish and maintain appropriate communication, particularly if either believes a patient's condition requires expertise beyond that of the resident. In such cases, it is the duty of the resident to inform the supervising physician of the urgency and scope of the patient's problem and to be particularly attentive to the patient's feelings. Should problems arise, the patient should already be aware of the resident's status and the fact that another physician may have to step in to care for the patient.

---

*The legal theory of vicarious liability states that responsibility for the acts of the resident lies not only with the resident, but also with the physician who directs or supervises him or her. Thus, the supervisor can be held legally responsible for the resident's actions. The physician's responsibility for the resident's actions arises out of the concept of an agency relationship. Under that concept, one person becomes the agent of a second person when the first person has been authorized to act for or represent the second. The partners in such a relationship are also referred to legally as "the master" and "the servant." The relevant legal doctrine—"Let the master speak," known as respondeat superior—holds that supervising physicians may be vicariously liable for the negligent acts of their residents.

This theory of law may also extend beyond the clinical faculty member to any physician who works with a resident, based on the legal concept of "the borrowed servant" or "the captain of the ship." Under these doctrines, one party may be liable for the acts of an employee of another if negligence occurs while the employee is under the first party's direction or control. (For further discussion, see Chapter II, pages 47–54.)

Resident-Patient Communications

Physicians always must clearly and honestly explain the nature of the services they can provide in terms that patients can comprehend. They must make sure that the patient has thoroughly understood the information that has been conveyed. Residents especially must always be sure to explain their status as a trainee to the patient, emphasizing that the care they provide is constantly supervised by the attending physician, who remains ultimately accountable for the care. The patient, of course, has the right to refuse treatment by a resident, but a good communicator can help the patient understand the advantages of receiving dual care, and a healthy, honest relationship can be the outgrowth of that exchange.

Always being willing to spend enough time with patients to answer their questions and address their concerns is an excellent way to demonstrate that the physician is their ally.

As a participant in the informed consent process, a resident must be aware of the steps to be followed: obtaining and disclosing all relevant facts; thoroughly explaining alternatives and reservations; ensuring that patients thoroughly comprehend information, advice, and instructions; and answering all questions. Proper implementation of these steps should make it possible to obtain a validly informed consent.

A resident's responsibilities do not necessarily end with treatment or surgery but also involve follow-up care, which may include follow-up visits and providing instructions to the patient. Ideally, all instructions to the patient should be detailed in writing and a copy placed in the patient's medical record for future reference.

Informed Consent

Informed consent is a legal doctrine that requires a physician to obtain consent for treatment rendered, an operation performed, and many diagnostic procedures. A complete discussion of consent and the process of informed consent is given earlier in this chapter (see pages 115–124).

Every resident should check hospital procedures to determine the kind of consent form that is preferred by the institution. Most importantly, every resident must be aware that all treatment must be backed by evidence of consent—whether oral or written, expressed or implied—granting permission for the resident to proceed, or evidence that the treatment was provided under circumstances in which consent could not be obtained.

Hospital Setting

The great majority of events leading to liability claims against physicians take place in the hospital setting. For that reason, it is especially important for residents to recognize their proper role in the treatment of hospitalized patients and in the institution's risk management program.

Typically, the resident plays a *supporting role* as part of a team functioning *under the supervision* of an attending physician. In some instances, however, the resident may function as a patient's primary physician. Whatever the circumstances, the resident must continually strive to achieve the dual goals of increasing patient safety and reducing risk.

From the resident's perspective, risk prevention in the hospital should begin with the resident's first encounter with a patient. Often it is the resident who is the first person to discuss with the patient the reason for the hospitalization. Therefore, it is the resident's responsibility to fully explain to the patient all of the information needed regarding hospitalization, including the reason for admission, the recommended treatment, treatment alternatives, and the potential risks and complications thereof.

Nothing is as likely to lead to litigation as the patient's surprise and disappointment with the treatment received. Therefore, as is the case with the supervising physician, it is vitally important for the resident to convey to the patient

IV / Risk Prevention

any possibility of complications or changes in expected outcome. For example, a patient who can be expected to experience fever, infection, or an extended hospital stay after an operation is far less likely to be disturbed by those events if the patient has been properly forewarned about their possibility. By the same token, a patient should always be advised if a procedure may entail risk or not achieve the desired result. Any patient who suffers a complication requires adequate time, attention, and information to understand what has occurred. Never is the resident's alertness and demonstration of concern for the patient's welfare more important than under such circumstances.

The resident should keep in mind the fact that many patients are under a great deal of stress and therefore may not be able to immediately grasp all the information being conveyed. For that reason, it may be helpful to summarize in writing information relayed verbally to give the patient and interested family members the opportunity to review and digest it. The original discussion also should be followed by a later opportunity to ask questions and clarify any misunderstandings or misconceptions that may remain.

Virtually every hospital, of course, has established rules and departmental protocols to ensure the delivery of uniformly high-quality patient care. In the interest of both preventing patient injury and minimizing the risk of liability, every member of the health care team must clearly understand the hospital's systems and protocols. Any failure on the part of the resident to comply with hospital policies is open to interpretation as a violation of the standard of care. Knowing, understanding, and complying with hospital policies is therefore as much in the interest of the resident as it is in that of the patient and hospital. Because national standards of care for specialists in training are being accepted increasingly, residents would also be wise to familiarize themselves with national guidelines, although hospital departmental protocols are likely to be more stringent than those national guidelines.

Risk Management in the Outpatient/Office Setting

Medical care is being provided in outpatient settings with increasing frequency. Because so many surgical procedures are now performed on an outpatient basis, a physician's initial contact with a patient today is more likely to occur in a physician's office than in the hospital. Whatever the setting, all contacts with patients should be conducted in the same manner that is expected in hospital practice, including the informed consent process and its essential discussion of risks, benefits, and alternatives to the proposed procedure or treatment, together with appropriate documentation of that discussion.

Patients also should be routinely informed of all test results, whether normal or abnormal, and these discussions noted in the patient's record. In addition, it is appropriate to provide the patient and/or family member with personalized instructions for continuing care. Such instructions also should be documented in the patient's record.

Resolving Ethical Issues

The American Medical Association principles of medical ethics provide that: "a physician shall in provision of appropriate patient care except in emergencies be free to choose whom to serve, with whom to associate, and the environment in which to provide medical services."

This principle gives physicians the right to choose their patients and refuse to render treatment that they consider morally or medically inappropriate. As supervised trainees, residents are not usually free to choose whom they will or will not see as patients. As a result, residents may be confronted with situations that require difficult decisions, situations such as being asked to perform a procedure that is beyond their expertise, encountering a complication they have not yet been trained to deal with, being asked to participate in or perform a procedure they are morally opposed to, or observing an impaired or incompetent physician attempting to provide patient care.

IV / Risk Prevention

Wise residents should be prepared to address such situations before they occur. A good way in which to do so is to determine whether the residency program, department, or hospital already has developed procedures for dealing with problem situations. Residents also should be well versed in departmental protocols for the various procedures that are performed in the department so that they know what should and should not be expected to occur. Another good idea is to obtain copies of departmental policies and procedures and the institution's bylaws to determine the proper chain of command within an institution. Finally, the resident should be aware that, whatever the formal protocols and chains of command, problem situations have arisen ever since medicine first was practiced; even where formal mechanisms to address such situations are not available, informal mechanisms may be.

If these protocols were to be exhausted, without providing a resolution of the problem, and if withholding care would result in greater harm to the patient than would attempting to provide it, residents should continue to treat the patient to the best of their ability, subsequently documenting in the medical record the steps that were taken to find substitute or additional care.

Today, given the many ethical questions that complicate even everyday medical practice, it is not unlikely that many residents will be forced to confront medical situations that raise personal moral issues of varying degrees. Where the potential exists for conflict, it is important to advise supervising physicians of the situation early in the residency program so that there is ample opportunity to make appropriate alternate arrangements. Any refusal on the part of the supervising physician to accede to a resident's request not to perform a procedure that is morally objectionable to the resident may be appealed throughout the appropriate chain of command.

Finding oneself caring for patients alongside a chemically impaired or incompetent physician poses another kind of moral dilemma for the resident. Lacking specific guidelines on how to proceed, any residents who may find themselves in these situations can only follow their own best judgment, remembering always that their patients' welfare is their overriding concern. Many institutions now have established formal channels through which an impaired or incompetent physician can be assisted in finding help.

Of course, an emergency situation is likely to preclude the resident's ability to consult with others about such a problem. In that event, if the physician's impairment is causing immediate harm to the patient, the resident may assert authority over that physician, and subsequently seek assistance from senior hospital staff.

References

1. Danner D: *Medical Malpractice: A Primer for Physicians*. Rochester, NY: The Lawyers Co-operative Publishing Co, 1988.

2. Palmisano DJ, Mang HJ, Jr.: *Informed Consent—A Survival Guide*. New Orleans: Invictus Publishing Company, 1987.

3. American College of Surgeons: *Patient Safety Manual: A Guide for Hospitals and Physicians to a Systematic Approach to Quality Assurance and Risk Management*. Written for the American College of Surgeons by Bader & Associates, Inc, Rockville, MD, 1985.

4. Brittain RS: The Practicing Surgeon's Perspective. Presented at Professional Liability Update, 75th Clinical Congress, American College of Surgeons, Atlanta, October 17, 1989.

5. Hirsh, HL: *Conferences on Legal-Medical Issues*. International Conferences of Huntington Station, New York, July 5-17, 1989.

6. Joint Commission on Accreditation of Healthcare Organizations: *Manual for Hospitals*. Chicago: Joint Commission on Accreditation of Healthcare Organizations, 1990.

7. Joint Commission on Accreditation of Healthcare Organizations: *Medical Staff Monitoring and Evaluation. Departmental Review*. Chicago: Joint Commission on Accreditation of Healthcare Organizations, 1988.

8. Committee to Study Medical Professional Liability and the Delivery of Obstetrical Care: *Medical Professional Liability and Delivery of Obstetrical Care*, vol 1. Washington, DC: National Academy Press, 1989.

IV / Risk Prevention

9. American College of Obstetricians and Gynecologists: *Professional Liability: A Resident's Survival Kit*. Washington, DC: American College of Obstetricians and Gynecologists, 1989.

V / CLAIMS MANAGEMENT

Editor's Note

Claims management is the process that occurs following the filing of a claim based on a patient's real or perceived injury. The surgeons who are the defendants in a medical malpractice action must become active participants in this process. This chapter discusses how a surgeon should choose and work with an attorney, particularly in the areas of deposition and trial. In addition, specific suggestions as to how a surgeon might handle various difficult situations are reviewed.

The fact that the surgeon should approach the process of giving a deposition with caution and confidence is emphasized. In addition to understanding the need to answer questions carefully, the surgeon must develop a sense of confidence through careful preparation to be fully knowledgeable about the data to be discussed. It is pointed out that this cautious but confident approach to the deposition must be combined with a disciplined demeanor that carefully avoids any expression of anger, irritation, or other types of inappropriate behavior.

It is also noted that the experience of going through a trial—especially if it is the surgeon's first exposure to that process, and if he or she is handicapped by a lack of familiarity with courtroom procedures—can be uncomfortable and unpleasant for the surgeon. The basic principles a surgeon should follow are described in detail.

In addition, the settlement process as one aspect of claims management is presented. Factors that should be considered by the defendant surgeon are described.

Finally, the important practical aspects of asset protection are discussed. Generic guidelines and common misconceptions are discussed, as is the suggestion that the surgeon might seek additional advice.

Surgeon-Attorney Relationship

General Considerations

Civil litigation is the legal process that ensues when a defendant receives a summons, usually together with another document, a complaint. This event gives legal notice that a lawsuit has been filed and that failure to respond will result in judgment by default.

For most physicians, participating in a lawsuit, especially as a defendant, is both an unfamiliar and uncomfortable process. Hence, the personal experience of the three authors of this section (MH, RR, and FS) is significant. MH is both a clinical cardiothoracic surgeon and an attorney (JD); he has recently written a book on professional liability.[1] RR is a neurosurgeon and a former chairman of the Professional Liability Committee of the American Association of Neurological Surgeons. FS, a clinical cardiothoracic surgeon and chairman of the Professional Liability Committee of the American College of Surgeons, has had an extensive personal experience with professional liability over the past 15 to 20 years. He has personally been the defendant in five jury trials, one of which was settled for an annuity, while the other four were all concluded with a jury verdict that found no malpractice whatsoever. These detailed personal experiences are described to provide the background for the general statements described in this chapter.

The usual procedure in a medical malpractice suit is for the plaintiff to file a formal document, the complaint or petition, which initiates the lawsuit and identifies the defendant(s)—in this situation, the physician. The complaint usually also states the nature of the claim or allegations and the relief requested, that is, monetary damages. Next, the defendant is served with the summons and complaint, and the defendant's answer or other formal response is required within a specific period of time. It is mandatory that the defendant physician notify the insurance company immediately, as almost always provided in the terms of the policy, so that preparations can begin for the timely filing of documents and other defense considerations. The documents and defense are handled by an attorney, with input from the defendant physician. The insurance company ordinarily arranges for the attorney, but if you are self-insured, you must obtain your own legal counsel.

Most physicians have little or no experience with courtroom trials. In the present medicolegal climate, this lack of experience is a serious handicap, for it makes the physician vulnerable to intimidation from unwarranted lawsuits. In some states, over 50 percent of lawsuits filed are ultimately decided as unwarranted. Only through the ability of the physician and his attorney to defend himself effectively, can he avoid intimidation from these unwarranted suits. On a more positive note, however, national data have shown repeatedly that a physician will win the majority of lawsuits in court, especially if careful preparation is made and there is no obvious malpractice.

With this knowledge that the courtroom experience is usually an unfamiliar one, but, with ample preparation, a successful result can usually be obtained, the importance of active participation by the physician with the attorney from the very onset of the lawsuit is obvious. The physician is an *active* participant, not simply passively following instructions from the attorney. This key principle is amplified further in the section entitled "Working with Your Attorney," but, in brief, legal evidence in a courtroom trial evolves from answers to the questions asked. As the

V / Claims Management

physician can only respond to the questions asked, deciding what *questions should be asked* to elucidate the significant data is a complex intellectual process, requiring both legal and medical expertise. As the attorney is not widely experienced in medicine, the active role of the physician in helping decide what questions should be asked during the trial is a key one, clearly emphasizing the importance of intensive preparation as well as active participation from the beginning. Simply passively awaiting instructions from the attorney to be told what to do next is grossly inadequate.

This intense active participation in the development of the defense requires a great deal of time, work, and intellectual effort, very similar to preparing for a board examination in a medical specialty. It requires hours of careful tabulation, analysis, and memorization of pertinent data to prepare for a board examination. It is worth every minute that is devoted to it.

As discussed in Chapter II, malpractice is a charge that the physician deviated from proper care of a patient and that this deviation resulted in injury to the patient. In medicine, answers to many major questions are simply unknown, such as the causes of cancer, atherosclerosis, or hypertension. Hence, a decision about the cause of an unexpected complication with a patient could be due to an unusual complication of the disease; a simple mishap, such as a fall in the bathroom; or malpractice. Often, the exact cause of the complication is unknown; so recognized experts sharply disagree.

It is a peculiarity of the American civil system of justice that such uncertainties are ultimately resolved by a jury trial. The United States is the only country in the entire world where such cases are resolved with a jury system, and decisions are made by laymen whose judgment must be based upon the conflicting testimony of so-called expert witnesses. This fact reiterates the importance of the active role of the physician because the decision in a trial is made both from the facts presented and from the jury's assessment of the credibility of opposing opinions presented by the plaintiff and the defendant. To repeat, using the principles outlined in this section, with careful preparation, combined with a significant amount of effort and study, a physician can win the vast majority of lawsuits.

Selecting an Attorney

In many instances, the insurance company responsible for the physician's professional liability insurance will select and assign an attorney. When this is done, the physician should meet with the attorney as soon as possible to develop an effective working relationship. It is particularly important for the physician to evaluate the competence of his attorney in professional liability, for experienced *defense* attorneys are less common than experienced attorneys for the plaintiff. Medical specialists evolve from years of special training in a residency training program designated for that specific purpose. In law, however, such specialized training programs do not exist; so the experience of individual attorneys must be acquired by personal experience. Hence, the previous experience of the attorney with professional liability is particularly important. Asking the attorney how often he or she has worked with other physicians, hospitals, and insurance companies in the same geographical area can be helpful. Subsequent conversations with these physicians may provide additional information. If, for unknown reasons, a young, inexperienced attorney recently graduated from law school, has been assigned, a more experienced attorney should usually be requested, for a great deal of the effectiveness of an attorney depends upon prior experience. Usually, the insurance company will make every effort to comply with the physician's request.

In large legal firms, a junior attorney may initially be assigned to evaluate a case, collect basic facts, and perhaps conduct the deposition, with the plan that a more senior attorney will conduct the trial. In general, except for initial fact-finding, this is a mediocre arrangement for the physi-

V / Claims Management

cian. The effectiveness of an attorney depends both upon his detailed familiarity with all of the data, as well as having developed a close working relationship with the physician. This enables him, in turn, to think of effective questions that should be asked as a result of events that occur during the trial. Simple legal expertise in the courtroom per se is inadequate.

When the physician has the option of selecting the attorney, the most effective source of information is to consult with colleagues who have had previous litigation experience. Inquire as to which attorneys they have used and what the litigation was.

There are several circumstances when a second attorney may be of value, including the following:

1. Lawsuits in which the damages grossly exceed the amount of your policy limits.

2. Any claim in which your insurance carrier has advised you that your insurance coverage is in debate or is questionable.

3. When, for whatever reason, you wish to settle a case and do not want a trial under any circumstances, or conversely, you insist upon a trial and your insurer is inclined to settle.

4. When your defense counsel feels another attorney would be helpful.

5. When you feel uncomfortable with your defense counsel, you may wish to retain your own attorney to become familiar with the case and advise you as to the quality of services being provided.

6. Whenever you suspect a conflict of interest exists, such as when your defense counsel is representing more than one party in the suit.

7. Any claim which would probably affect your licensure or staff privileges.

Working with Your Attorney

As repeatedly stated in this chapter, the physician must be an active participant in the entire litigation process. This involves a large amount of planning and work, similar to studying for a board examination in a specialty. This includes hours of careful tabulation, analysis, and memorization of pertinent data. The major pretrial activities that allow both parties to discover information about the opponent's case are called *discovery*. These activities include written interrogatories; request for production of documents; physical and mental examinations; and deposition. Interrogatories consist of a series of questions submitted by one party to the opponents and must be answered in writing, under oath, within a certain time period. Responding to such questions obviously requires consultation with your attorney. Other fact-finding activities may or may not be used, depending upon the judgment of the attorneys. A most important discovery procedure, however, is the *deposition*, discussed in the following section. This has been called the plaintiff attorney's "deadly weapon."

The legal evidence in a lawsuit is principally the patient's hospital chart and the physician's office records. As these are legal evidence, they cannot be used as personal notes. As a first step, the physician should obtain a personal copy of the entire hospital chart, no matter if it is a few hundred pages in length and requires several hundred dollars to duplicate. Also, the physician's entire office records should be duplicated so they can be marked, indexed, and notations made as a personal working copy. The original records, of course, must be submitted at trial and *cannot* be marked or altered in any way.

The entire hospital chart should be carefully scanned, page by page, with appropriate notes and indices made for reference. This is both time-consuming and laborious, but highly effective. Considerable harm to a physician's case can occur at trial if the plaintiff attorney questions the

V / Claims Management

physician about data in the patient's chart with which he is not familiar. Hence, complete familiarity with the record, including all progress notes, nurses' notes, laboratory findings, and other significant data should be obtained by careful study and review. These data must then be memorized, similar to preparing for an examination. Only by being completely familiar with the data can a physician answer questions effectively and consider what points should be developed at trial in the cross-examination process.

A similar, but less laborious, process should be done with all office records, committing the key data to memory so potentially adverse questions can be effectively answered. Unless the physician owns and studies a personal copy of both the hospital chart and the office records, an effective review cannot be done. The hospital chart and records cannot be marked, cross-indexed, and used for personal purposes.

This tabulation and study of pertinent data should be done before the first detailed meeting between the physician and the attorney. This first meeting is educational both for the physician and the attorney, each learning from the other the key issues in the defense of the case. The amount of time required to accomplish this cannot be predicted with any certainty; so a large block of time should be set aside, preferably in the late afternoon or early evening. Scheduling a short meeting during the working hours of a busy day is woefully inadequate, inviting disaster. Although uncommon, a physician should never accept restriction on the amount of time used in preparation by the attorney. The attorney is functioning as the physician's employee through the insurance company, and will be reimbursed whether the case is won or lost. The physician, however, is on trial and stands to lose both money and reputation; so he should not only allocate as much time as possible for preparation, but insist that the attorney do likewise. In most instances, the attorney is more than willing to devote all the time needed, while the physician may be reluctant. This must be avoided.

Expert witnesses, both in the subject being litigated and in courtroom procedures, are essential for an effective defense. The defendant physician should assist his attorney in identifying and contacting appropriate experts, based on personal knowledge, or information supplied by colleagues. Once chosen, the expert witness must be given a complete copy of the records and any other available information. Subsequently, the attorney may wish to arrange a joint meeting with the physician and the expert witness to discuss various aspects of the case.

How many meetings between the physician and his attorney will be required before a deposition will vary with the complexity of the case, ranging from one or two meetings to several. The number of meetings required is immaterial, as long as complete and thorough preparation is done.

The Deposition

General Considerations

The deposition is a standard legal procedure commonly used before a courtroom trial. It is primarily a fact-finding inquiry by the plaintiff attorney to permit him or her to discover any facts that would be applicable in the case being litigated.

In general, this is a one-sided process for the plaintiff, for the plaintiff attorney can ask a wide range of questions, while the defendant physician can simply answer them as best he can unless his attorney objects. The physician should answer questions as concisely as he can without elaboration. He should not elaborate in a futile attempt to educate the plaintiff attorney and, hopefully, have the suit dismissed. Theoretically, the defendant physician is required to answer, as best as possible, all appropriate questions. In unusual circumstances, if a physician refuses to answer a question, the plaintiff attorney can adjourn the deposition and request a court order requiring the physician to answer.

The deposition is usually conducted in a conference room of one of the law offices of one of the attorneys, either the plaintiff or the defense. The atmosphere is semi-formal; participants include the plaintiff attorney, the defendant physician, the defendant attorney, attorneys for any co-defendants, and a court reporter. Although the atmosphere may seem somewhat relaxed, the physician should take the entire procedure very soberly and seriously, for he has little to gain, but may seriously injure his case with unplanned improper testimony. The answers by the defendant are given under oath and become legal evidence that can be introduced subsequently at trial. If contradictory statements are made at trial, the physician's statements in the deposition can be used to either impair his credibility or actually impeach his testimony. Hence, the deposition is essentially a "mini-trial" with the potential for little to gain, but a lot to lose.

As neither a judge nor a jury is present, the plaintiff's attorney is permitted a wide latitude of questioning, far more so than at trial. His only restriction is that the line of questioning could conceivably lead to "admissible evidence." One casual description of the overall procedure is a "fishing-expedition."

Preparation for Deposition

As described in the preceding section regarding the physician working with the attorney, detailed study and preparation are essential, requiring a lot of time and effort. The entire procedure should be viewed with the same gravity as proceeding with a courtroom trial.

The physician should obtain a personal copy of the patient's entire hospital record, as well as a copy of all office notes and other data. The original office records and hospital chart are legal evidence and must not be altered in any way. However, from the personal copies, indices can be constructed, notations made, and the data assembled for reference, review, and memorization. These working copies should *not* be brought to the deposition, because any material present at the deposition may be requested by the plaintiff attorney and used by him accordingly. Hence, the physician responds from memory to questions from the attorney, referring to the hospital record or the official office notes as necessary. It is obvious, therefore, that careful analysis and memorization of data beforehand is crucial.

The importance of detailed planning between the physician and his attorney was emphasized in the preceding section. A meeting immediately preceding the deposition is essential, again reviewing key points that may develop in response to the questions that will probably be asked.

Legal Considerations

In planning for a deposition, it is important to emphasize what is and what is not malpractice. Malpractice is defined as a significant deviation from the standard of care, with the added stipulation that this deviation caused injury to the patient. The standard of care is the quality of care that would be given by a reasonably competent practitioner in that specialty, not exceptional care. An error in judgment, unless significantly inferior to that of the usual community physician, does not by itself constitute malpractice.

It must clearly be demonstrated that this deviation from the standard of care caused injury to the patient. The deviation, per se, is not malpractice unless a demonstrated injury occurred as a consequence. Hence, the physician should rarely, if ever, *admit* that his deviation from a standard of care caused the patient injury. This is the approach that will be pursued by the expert witness for the plaintiff. If the physician under oath agrees that his care caused the injury, he essentially has become the expert witness against himself.

Similarly, the physician should restrict his answers as far as possible to the care he rendered to the patient in question, not the broad subject of the disease being treated. To do otherwise has him assuming the role of the expert witness. Broad, general statements by the physician to demonstrate his breadth of knowledge may subsequently be used against him.

Maintaining a Professional Demeanor

The physician should maintain a formal, professional demeanor while answering questions slowly, thoughtfully, and concisely. He should neither be overtly hostile or combative, nor appear careless or bored. The intense, sober concentration required is somewhat similar to participating in a chess tournament. Comments or questions, such as jokes, gratuitous compliments, abuses or insults, should be viewed as potential distractions that could interrupt the physician's concentration on the subject, and hence, should be briefly acknowledged or simply ignored. It is most important that the physician discipline himself beforehand to not become angry or irritated, no matter the provocation, even though some questions may naturally irritate, annoy, or anger; all of these emotional reactions distract the intensity of thinking. Becoming angry might be fully justified, but the impaired concentration that evolves can lead to improper or hazardous answers to subsequent questions that are then part of the legal testimony. The plaintiff attorney thus benefits, not the physician. Under no circumstances should the physician attempt to argue with the plaintiff counsel.

After a puzzling or complex question, the physician may pause to provide time for his attorney to object. If his attorney objects, the physician should simply listen until the objection is decided. Similarly, if the physician becomes fatigued or distracted from a long series of questions, he can request a recess.

Answering Questions

The defendant physician can only answer questions asked by the plaintiff attorney. He, cannot ask questions and, in general, cannot comment, except in answer to a specific question.

The two key requirements for effective testimony at a deposition are a thorough familiarity with the pertinent data, coupled with an understanding of what to answer, how to answer, and what not to answer. In many ways, what not to say and what not to answer are almost equal in importance to what answers are given.

Answers to questions should be simple, thoughtful, and specific, based upon written statements in the patient's chart or the physician's notes. The most concrete answer is one which can be validated by what has been documented in the notes in the hospital chart or the office records.

A second type of answer is based on *specific memory*; a physician clearly remembers the events about which the question is asked. Usually, specific memory answers are based on recent events or vivid circumstances that the physician remembers clearly.

Questions about events in the remote past that are neither documented in the record nor remembered specifically should be answered in general terms, such as, "My routine practice in such circumstances is _____." There is certainly no realistic expectation that a physician should remember such details. Under no circumstances should the physician guess or speculate as to what he specifically did with a patient. Such statements are of dubious validity, and are often contradictory. Simply answer, "My usual routine is _____ ; otherwise I don't remember."

Answer the Question—Do Not Lecture

It should be repeatedly emphasized that the deposition process of a defendant physician is a broad-ranging fact-finding inquiry by the plaintiff's attorney to discover material that he might use subsequently at trial. This is primarily for the plaintiff's benefit; the physician has little to gain, but unwittingly can harm his case by gratuitously providing important information previously unknown to the plaintiff. He should not attempt to elaborate and impress the plaintiff counsel with his knowledge and skill, hoping that the case will be terminated. Similarly, he should restrain his natural instincts to teach or explain and simply answer the question. It should be repeated again and again that the physician should only answer the question, not volunteer information, attempt to educate the attorney, or correct erroneous statements unless absolutely necessary.

Complex, Deceptive Questions

The professional skill of the plaintiff attorney in many ways depends upon the nature of the questions that he can formulate. Answers to these questions create the legal evidence upon which the case is developed. A wide range of complex, misleading, or deceptive questions can be utilized in an attempt to mislead or trap the unwary physician. Many good examples of hazardous questions are discussed in the 1988 publication by Danner, *Medical Malpractice: A Primer for Physicians.* [2] Unless the question is clear and the answer obvious, the physician can simply state, "I don't understand," "I don't know," or "I don't remember." Alternately, he may ask that the question be rephrased.

Several examples of misleading or tricky questions are described in the following paragraphs.

"Yes or No" A complex question may be followed with a firm request in a dictatorial tone, "Simply answer, yes or no!" Such questions are designed so that either answer is hazardous. An exaggerated example of such a question is, "Have you stopped beating your wife?" The proper response to such questions is to simply reply that the question must be rephrased, as it cannot be answered with a simple "yes" or "no."

Ambiguous Questions that are ambiguous can be interpreted in different ways; these should simply be rejected with the request that the question be rephrased or, "I don't understand." A so-called leading question is one in which the answer sought is embodied in the question. For example, "As this wound infection resulted from absence of prophylactic antibiotics, should antibiotics be routinely given?" Answering the question as formulated agrees with a key point that the wound infection resulted from lack of antibiotics. This is essentially admitting that a deviation from a standard of practice caused the patient's injury. The physician has unwittingly testified against himself.

Hypothetical Be particularly wary of a hypothetical question, such as, "Let's assume such and such." This, in essence, is a discussion of the subject, not the patient, and is best avoided by restricting comments to the care of the particular patient. Expounding on the subject of the disease being treated is seldom helpful and has serious hazards. A similar question may be initiated with a casual, "Well, off the record, let's assume such and such."

Another deceptive phrase is the preamble, "With a reasonable degree of medical certainty, such and such." This type of statement is hazardous because it can be subjected to a wide variety of interpretations. For example, "With a reasonable degree of medical certainty, vomiting is consistent with a diagnosis of appendicitis." Such a statement is true, but misleading. Vomiting is also consistent with innumerable disorders, such as cerebellar tumors or pregnancy. It is far more precise to answer in terms of probability, such as 5 to 20 percent, than with the statement, "Approximately _____ percent of patients with appendicitis experience vomiting."

Authoritative Textbook Another common trap is to ask if a physician recognizes a textbook as "authoritative." This should very rarely be answered as "Yes" because then any deviation of the physician's performance from what is recorded in the textbook is an admission of deviation from authoritative practice. Textbooks, in general, should simply be described as helpful references, but only one of many sources of information. Some parts are helpful, some are not.

The Trial

General Considerations

A courtroom trial is very different from virtually any activity a physician normally does in the practice of medicine. Most of a physician's work is with the diagnosis and treatment of a patient's disease, trying to either cure the problem or make the patient more comfortable. A courtroom trial, however, is an adversarial experience in which allegations are made and facts are presented, but sharp, even bitter, controversy often develops about the significance and interpretation of the facts, often with legal maneuvers that can distort their meaning or suppress their presentation altogether. It may be a brutal, depressing experience for both the patient plaintiff and the physician defendant. More than once it has been described as "civilized man's answer to war." A detailed discussion of the psychological trauma attendant to a trial is described in the final chapter of this book.

A particularly unique aspect of the experience is that the courtroom procedure is not only a search for the facts, but often includes different forms of attacks on the reputation of the defendant physician. There are four well-known methods for doing this. The most obvious and most common is to *challenge his competence*. If the physician is clearly well-trained and competent, a second avenue of attack is to *charge the physician with carelessness*. "He is well-trained, but simply so busy he can't pay attention to details," and "Everyone makes mistakes!" A third method, discussed in more detail in the section entitled "Maintaining a Professional Demeanor," is to challenge his compassion, portraying him as an indifferent, noncaring, wealthy entrepreneur.

The fourth method, highly effective with contradictory testimony, is to *impair credibility*. This is usually done by demonstrating inconsistencies in testimony, especially between the pretrial deposition and the court testimony. Blatant, overt dishonesty is rarely charged.

Hence, the physician can anticipate attack and abuse in any or all of these four categories. His type of response, discussed in the subsequent section entitled "Maintaining a Professional Demeanor," is crucial. The arousing of emotions in a witness by intimidation, provocation, or guilt evocation is a well-established questioning technique. No matter how irritating or unwarranted abusive statements may be, under no circumstances must the physician become visibly angry. Questions may be designed primarily to provoke anger, which, no matter how justified, may ultimately harm the physician and help the plaintiff.

On a more positive note, with careful planning and full knowledge of pertinent data concerning the case, combined with an understanding of courtroom procedures, the physician can win at trial the majority of all suits in which there is no obvious malpractice. As stated in the introduction to this section, one of the authors (FS) has personally been the defendant through five separate jury trials, settling one for an annuity for a brain-injured child with no admission of guilt, while the other four were all concluded unanimously in the defendant's favor.

Planning and Preparation

During the trial of a complex, potentially hazardous lawsuit, the physician should virtually stop the practice of medicine and plan on being in court 80 to 90 percent of the time. Well-meaning advice, such as, "You will be called as little as possible so you can continue to work with your

V / Claims Management

patients," may be reassuring but can be tantamount to disaster.

Being physically present in court most of the time is essential for two major reasons. First, an important factor influencing the credibility of a physician's statements before a jury is the personality of the physician. In brief, "Is he the type of physician that they respect and would seek for their personal illness?" "Does he seem compassionate and concerned that the patient sustained an unforeseen complication, or does he seem irritated and angry at what he considers an unjust assault on his good intentions and reputation?" The proper demeanor must be conveyed by appearance as well as by words; so there is no substitute for being regularly seen in the courtroom, soberly observing and listening to everything that is said.

The second major reason for being present is to listen carefully to all testimony in order to detect statements that could be useful in the defense. In complex cases, transcripts of the testimony given in the earlier days of the trial can be obtained and studied in detail. The basic charge is against the quality of medical care and that the alleged deviation from the accepted standard of care resulted in injury to the patient. The attorney is an expert in legal matters while the physician is not; the physician, however, is knowledgeable in medicine. Hence, the physician should carefully listen for erroneous or contradictory statements about medical facts or events that can subsequently be examined by his attorney when he questions either the plaintiff, his expert witness, or the defendant physician. He is not only looking for key points but trying to help decide what questions his attorney could use to demonstrate the contradictory or erroneous statements. His attorney, of course, is the final judge of the best approach to follow.

This is an intense intellectual process, concentrating carefully on the evolving events and looking for clues that could be helpful. The senior author of this section (FS) found major clues in two of four trials that were subsequently developed by his attorney and clearly played a decisive role in discrediting the testimony of the expert witness for the plaintiff. This intense intellectual process is the principal reason that a physician must be a very active participant in the entire legal proceedings, starting from the receipt of the subpoena to the conclusion of the courtroom trial.

The basic preparation for the trial is essentially the accumulation and careful study of all pertinent data, already described in the sections entitled "Working with Your Attorney" and "Preparation for Deposition." Hence, this information will not be repeated here, but the intensity of the work and intellectual effort is almost identical to that involved in planning for an oral examination for specialty Board certification.

The close surgeon-attorney relationship that was initiated at the beginning of the case, and further developed through the pretrial deposition, is crucial at this time. In complex cases, the physician and the attorney need to meet and discuss each day the developments and the plans for the subsequent day, either during the day in court or that evening. The physician virtually retires from the practice of medicine during this time.

Maintaining a Professional Demeanor

The importance of maintaining a formal, professional demeanor, no matter the irritation or abuse, cannot be overstated. This was emphasized in the preceding section, "The Deposition." During the deposition, a calm, sober demeanor was necessary to avoid distraction from the clarity of thinking. In the courtroom trial, this is even more important because of the emotional impact the appearance and attitude of the physician may have on the jury. The demeanor of the physician should be that which a juror would respect and admire. He is appropriately formal, courteous, not smiling; the events are neither funny nor humorous, especially to the injured patient. He is neither unduly humble or agreeable, compliant or subservient, nor fearful or hostile. He maintains his courteous professional demeanor no matter what abuse, admirably demonstrating "grace under pressure." The intensity of concentration displayed, ignoring distractions, is similar to participating in a chess tournament.

The four major aspects of a physician's reputation that may be questioned, are competence, care, compassion, and credibility. All of these should be embodied in the physician's demeanor and behavior.

Competence is displayed by answers that are clear and certain, expressed with confidence without equivocation or obvious arrogance.

Care is shown by demeanor, thinking carefully, answering slowly and deliberately, avoiding flip statements, snappy answers, or brisk retorts.

Compassion is exemplified by the overall behavior in court, demonstrating a serious appropriate concern for the distress of the patient that led to the lawsuit, rather than displaying anger or irritation at what he considers unjust accusations.

A physician's *credibility* is demonstrated primarily by the consistency of his statements, stating clearly what he knows, what he does not know, or does not remember.

Under no circumstances can the defendant physician afford to become visibly angry. With particularly abusive questions, he should pause to give opportunity for his attorney to object. If an objection occurs, he, of course, remains silent until the judge makes a ruling.

Testimony

A basic principle of effective testimony is termed *persuasive speaking*, with positive, clear comments that underline their credibility. Answering questions in court is quite different from answering the same questions during the deposition. In the deposition, the goal is to answer questions without providing excessive information to the plain-

tiff attorney. Hence, questions are answered clearly and as briefly as possible. In court, however, the physician is speaking directly to the jury, a lay audience who must interpret opposing statements both by what is said and by their assessment of the credibility of the speaker. The physician should speak directly to the jury, with eyeball-to-eyeball contact that connotes sincerity and credibility. This type of behavior is diametrically opposite to that of the aloof indifferent physician who unemotionally recites the facts in answer to a question. When feasible, answers should be given that can be elaborated upon if further understanding can be helpful. For example, if an elaborate answer is useful, a direct question can be answered as "Yes, for five distinct reasons. These are as follows: _____ , _____ , _____ , _____ , and _____ ."
This type of elaboration, of course, is not given at the deposition, but is valuable at trial, not only indicating the importance of the data, but the physician's overall knowledge of the subject. Often, the plaintiff attorney will try to interrupt such answers. If necessary, the defense attorney can provide another opportunity for the physician to elaborate during his cross-examination of the physician.

Repetition

Important facts in the physician's defense should be repeated as frequently as possible during answers to different questions. The jurors are instructed not to make notes; so frequent repetition of important facts can be valuable.

Clarity of Communication

This is an additional important vehicle for creating better understanding by the jurors. When feasible, a blackboard or other visual aids may be useful to illustrate complex medical issues, not only clarifying the point in question but also demonstrating the physician's overall knowledge of the subject.

Specific answers to questions are identical to those described in the section entitled "The Deposition." That section should be read in planning for a trial, as some of the same guidelines are applicable in both situations. In brief, the most concrete specific answers are those that are documented in the patient's hospital chart or the office records. Precise answers may also be possible for events for which the physician has a clear and specific memory. Certain events in the distant past can usually only be partly recalled. In no instance should the physician speculate; such speculation is not only of dubious value, but easily leads to contradictory statements. The best answer is to describe "my usual practice" or to simply state that "I don't recall."

The same advice given about complex deceptive questions in the section on deposition testimony is, of course, equally applicable in the courtroom.

Questions are usually asked about textbooks. Such questions include what textbooks are used, which are "authoritative," and similar questions. The physician may comment on opinions in the different textbooks, displaying not only his own familiarity with the material, but the independence of his own thinking. The trap to avoid, of course, is accepting any textbook in its entirety as being "authoritative." This can usually be answered in general terms such as, "Like several excellent textbooks, some are helpful in some areas, but not in others. No one is completely authoritative."

The Plaintiff Expert Witness

This section concerns the responsibility of the defendant physician in analyzing and, hopefully, discrediting the qualifications of the expert witness for the plaintiff, a key element in the entire case. Guidelines for the *behavior* of the physician when he testifies as an expert witness, not as a defendant, are not described in this section, but are detailed in three publications (two from the Professional Liability Committee of the American College of Surgeons) published in 1988 and 1989.[3-5]

The testimony of the expert witness for the plaintiff is crucial for the plaintiff's case, for the jury, as laymen, cannot determine independently the quality of the medical care, but must evaluate the conflicting testimonies of the expert witnesses for the plaintiff and the defense. The potential for serious abuse currently exists in the legal *qualifications* for an expert witness, some of which have been corrected in a few states with specific remedial legislation. This subject has been discussed in detail in two recent publications from the Professional Liability Committee of the American College of Surgeons.[3, 5]

In brief, the decision as to what qualifications are required for an expert witness is a legal one, not a medical one. A medical organization can describe appropriate qualifications but these are simply recommendations with no legal authority unless enforced by the court system.

The current abuses with "unqualified" expert witnesses arose from difficulty in past years of finding any expert witness of any kind for the plaintiff. The broad, excessively liberal rule arose that any person with a medical degree might qualify to testify, regardless of specialty or background.[1] Improvements have occurred, but serious defects remain. At present, in many states, a physician may testify in a case, even though his or her training in that specialty is meager, and the physician may not have actively practiced the specialty in years, perhaps never.

The background of this rule is described in some detail in order to explain that many "experts" have limited training and experience with the specific medical condition being litigated. In some states, the expert witness is known in advance; so a deposition may be taken or a search of his background can be made to determine what type of testimony he has given in previous similar trials. In other states, however, the identity of the expert witness is not known until he appears in court to take the witness stand.

Usually, from experience, the "professional" expert witness has acquired an imposing presence on the witness stand, appearing wise, reflective, and scholarly, a true "expert." This presence may be accompanied by an orotund, authoritative manner of speaking, designed, like the theater, to convey the impression of authority and wisdom. However, the simple fact that the plaintiff has employed a professional expert with little, if any, experience in the matter at hand can be exploited with great benefit by a vigorous cross-examination by the defendant's attorney.

The defendant physician has a key role in this analysis of the knowledge and reasoning of the plaintiff expert, for his attorney cannot judge his medical knowledge or the validity of his conclusions. This may be one of the most critical elements in the entire trial. If the physician knows the data and the subject in detail, erroneous or unsound conclusions by the expert may become apparent. The basic question is, "Are the conclusions supported by the pertinent data?" These analyses can subsequently be used by the defense attorney in cross-examination to seriously discredit the qualifications of the expert. To repeat, this type of analysis can best be done by the physician, knowing both the data and listening to the testimony; possibly, it could be done by the expert witness for the defendant, but he usually has not heard the majority of the preceding testimony.

One of the authors (FS) has personally used this approach effectively in two major trials, both of which reached a verdict in favor of the defendant.

One suit concerned a plastic surgeon who underwent cardiac surgery for a prosthetic valve replacement. Subsequently, a mild diplopia and Horner's syndrome evolved; the surgeon retired on total disability with the claim that his impaired vision prevented him from performing surgery. A CAT (computerized axial tomogram) scan of the brain demonstrated a linear opacity in the wall of one of the two vertebral arteries proximal to their junction at the base of the brain to form the basilar artery. The charge was that a fragment of vascular catheter (an "angiocath") had broken off at operation and embolized to the vertebral artery, even though there was no record of such an episode, nor had a similar episode ever been recorded. The most probable explanation was that the eccentric opacity in the wall of the vertebral artery was a form of calcification. Despite the dubious validity of the entire charge, the case, over a period of years, proceeded to trial.

During the trial, a visual display of the anatomy of the base of the brain showed the anatomical course of the vertebral and basilar arteries and their relationship to the cranial nerves innervating the musculature of the eye. The plaintiff expert witness testified that the opacity in one vertebral artery caused the neurologic deficit. On studying the anatomical drawings, it became apparent that an opacity in the wall of one vertebral artery, regardless of type or source, could not possibly injure a cranial nerve to the eye as the cranial nerves for the eye muscles (III, IV, and VI) arise from the brain stem at the level of the basilar artery, not at the level of the vertebral artery more proximally. Incredibly enough, this simple anatomical fact had not been recognized previously by several consultants over a period of years. Its subsequent emphasis was clearly significant in reaching a favorable verdict.

Another example occurred in a trial in which the charge was that the use of the antibiotic clindamycin (Cleocin) following a cardiac operation led to pseudomembranous colitis, severe dehydration, and shock. The patient survived with a temporary ileostomy, followed by colon reconstruction. The cardiac operation had been performed before the relationship between clindamycin and enterocolitis was widely known; the origin of the disease from *Clostridium difficile* had not been established. The expert witness for the plaintiff stoutly asserted that the patient had been neglected for days with improper fluid replacement, resulting in progressive dehydration and shock resembling cholera. The neglected fluid replacement over a period of days that produced severe dehydration and shock was denounced in strong, theatrical terms as malpractice.

V / Claims Management

Having studied the patient's hospital chart in detail, it was known that proper hydration had been given, the patient's fluid balance was satisfactory, and the blood urea nitrogen was normal. The blood urea nitrogen had been measured daily. Knowing that the blood urea nitrogen is quickly elevated as a result of a decrease in renal blood flow produced by dehydration, the defense attorney, by simply questioning on cross-examination whether the expert witness knew what the blood urea nitrogen was before he made such sweeping conclusions about days of neglect from improper fluid replacement, quickly revealed the witness' carelessness and seriously impaired his credibility. A successful verdict for the defendant was soon forthcoming.

To summarize, the expert witness for the plaintiff plays a key role in the entire case. He must demonstrate to the jury that the case provided by the defendant physician was "substandard" and that this deviation from accepted medical practice caused the plaintiff's injury. If his testimony can be discredited with proper questions on cross-examination, the case for the defense is greatly strengthened. Effective questions by the defense attorney may demonstrate lack of knowledge of the specialty, a careless review of the patient's record, or improper conclusions from the data available. As said earlier, this careful analysis is a crucial responsibility for the defendant physician; it can seldom, if ever, be done by anyone else unless he knows the data and the entire case thoroughly and has heard the majority of preceding testimony.

Complaining, after the trial, of deceptive, misleading, or inaccurate testimony by the expert witness, which may seem downright fraudulent, is virtually futile. The entire court has the responsibility for accepting the qualifications of the expert witness and his testimony. Unless this testimony is discredited *at trial*, unless gross perjury can be proved later, virtually nothing can be done.

Settlement

Settlement, an important part of the litigation process, usually occurs in the pretrial phase, but also may occur at subsequent stages of the lawsuit. Although no exact figures are available, it is estimated that from 90 to 97 percent of all civil litigation, including medical malpractice actions, ends in settlement or dismissal before trial.

A settlement made between the parties to an incident or a claim involved in a lawsuit is an agreement that resolves the legal dispute. It results in final disposition of a case without a decision on the merits of the case. Usually, payment is made to the plaintiff in exchange for a release, which is a legal document that absolves the defendant from all past, present, and future liability in connection with the incident or claim.

Most releases specifically state that settlement by the defendant does not constitute an admission of fault. The provisions of some malpractice insurance policies permit the insurer to settle without the concurrence of the insured physician, but, usually, the physician has some control over the process.

Considerations in Settlement

The process of settlement may follow one of many possible courses. The probability of winning or losing at trial, as well as a number of other considerations, must be carefully balanced in deciding whether or not to settle. These other considerations include the presence or absence of legally actionable negligence; the severity of the patient's injury and disability; the type and quality of available experts who will face each other on behalf of the plaintiff and defendant in "the battle of the experts"; the location, or venue, of the lawsuit—for example, whether it is to be tried in a conservative rural area or a liberal, more plaintiff-oriented urban center; factors that might engender sympathy in the jurors and influence them to award large sums for pain and suffering; the adequacy or inadequacy of the available record; and the presence of alterations of the record, which might result in loss of an otherwise defensible case.

Other increasingly important considerations relating to settlements are malpractice reporting requirements, which vary somewhat from state to state. Under these reporting provisions, all payments resulting from settlements and awards (or, in some cases, payments that exceed certain sums) must be reported to data banks, to state licensing authorities, or to other administrative bodies. Mandatory reporting is required, for example, by the National Practitioner Data Bank, which has been activated. The exact effect of mandatory reporting as instituted by the Data Bank legislation is still not clear. The practical effect of such legislation, however, is likely to discourage settlement, particularly in cases involving minor injuries, because defendants may choose to chance a favorable jury outcome and thus avoid the negative implications of the reporting process.

Factors Favoring Settlement

The law favors settlement. As a general rule, settlement promotes judicial economy, expedites claim resolution, removes the uncertainties inherent in a trial, conserves the parties' resources, is socially desirable in that it ends discord, and potentially could minimize dissatisfaction with the legal process.

Each participant in a suit has reason to prefer settlement. The *judge*, eager to clear the court calendar and dispose of cases, may require the parties to participate in a pretrial settlement conference. The *insurance carrier* wishes to limit the cost of a defense, establish a fixed sum of payment, and avoid exposure to the uncertainties of a jury trial and the possibility that it will result in a large award to the plaintiff. The *plaintiff's attorney* considers settlement a victory inasmuch as it ensures compensation for the client and for the attorney's time and effort, while avoiding the litigation lottery that a trial represents. The *defense attorney* also wishes to avoid the uncertainty of a jury verdict.

Finally, in reaching a settlement, the defendant physician avoids the danger of a verdict in excess of the physician's insurance coverage, an increasingly important consideration inasmuch as the severity of claims is increasing, while the availability of excess insurance coverage is diminishing. Settlement also saves the time and energy demanded by the litigation process.

How Settlement Is Reached

Parties have great latitude in working out a means to resolve their justiciable controversies, so that many disputes can be resolved without prolonged, expensive, and emotionally traumatic litigation. The process includes many possibilities, some within or a part of the litigation process itself. On the other hand, a number of extrajudicial possibilities are available which do not require the usual litigation formalities.

Incident Settlement

Settlement of an incident may occur when the possibility of a claim is first identified. Here, the physician may play a primary role, although attorneys are also essential. The insurance carrier must, of course, always be notified and be in agreement and willing to participate. The hospital risk manager should also be involved, or at least notified, if the incident occurred in a hospital. Settlement will then depend on the response of the insurer, the hospital, and the parties, and may include treatment of the patient at no cost in exchange for release, or some amount of compensation to the patient.

Settlement After Lawsuit

After a lawsuit is filed, the attorneys play a primary role. Plaintiff attorneys frequently make a monetary demand upon the defense attorney, to which the defense attorney then responds with rejection, acceptance, or a counter-offer. Negotiations may continue until the parties arrive at an acceptable settlement figure. Demands or counter-offers can be made at any time, even if settlement negotiations have previously broken down. The insurance carrier, of course, plays a critical role and retains authority to negotiate settlements. The defense attorney may only accept a settlement demand or make a counter-offer with the consent of the insurance carrier. The defendant physician's role depends upon the provisions of the insurance policy. Thus, it is important that physicians be aware of the terms of their respective policies. Settlement continues to be a factor, even after a verdict has been rendered and during the appeals process, when both parties will attempt to minimize their losses and replace continuing uncertainty with a definitive outcome.

Although settlement usually occurs within the litigation process following direct negotiations among the attorneys, the judge may also take a direct role, which may take the form of informal discussions or suggestions, in an attempt to resolve disputes. Beyond this, the judge may actually become a mediator, may speak directly to the parties (as well as to the attorneys), and may require and structure conferences to attempt resolution.

Alternative settlement techniques are also encouraged by the courts. These include mandatory non-binding arbitration; mediation designed to encourage parties to identify the differences and resolve them; summary jury trials in which each attorney presents his or her case to a jury drawn from the regular jury pool, and where the subsequent verdict is then used in settlement negotiations; and the use of court-appointed neutral experts, which are permitted by federal courts and most state courts, but which have not been widely used.

Other Methods of Resolving Controversies

There are also other methods for resolving disputes, not usually considered part of the settlement process, but which nonetheless result in expedited extra-judicial resolution of a claim. These methods consist of procedures used in litigation, as well as others not a part of the litigation process, and include settlement of cases without filing a lawsuit; mini-trials based on procedures to which the parties agree; binding arbitration; conciliation or mediation, which involve the assistance of impartial third parties; fact-finding by another party for identification of issues; private judging, where the dispute is submitted to a former or retired judge for resolution; and a combination of the various methods.

Conclusions

Realistic and objective assessment of the option of settlement at any stage of the claim, either before or after the filing of a lawsuit, is a continuing consideration. This multifaceted, ongoing process should operate to expeditiously resolve an indefensible or perhaps a borderline defensible claim. A final decision should be made objectively, based on the factors previously noted, as well as on the advice of the defense and personal attorneys.

Protecting One's Assets

Strategies for dealing with one's personal finances should include timely planning for the protection of past, present, or future assets from judgment creditors or creditors in bankruptcy proceedings. Such considerations are essential, since nonexempt assets are available to creditors for the satisfaction of a debtors' obligations and are thus at risk to the extent an award for compensatory or punitive damages is not covered by insurance.

The risk of a judgment in excess of insurance coverage is particularly evident in the increasing severity of jury awards in medical malpractice cases, where average awards in excess of $1 million, ranging as high as $54.8 million, have been reported in 1989 and 1990. The risk is enhanced by the declining availability of excess " umbrella" coverage for malpractice liability and is further reflected in the continuing high cost of malpractice insurance. An evaluation of this risk and its potential consequences includes consideration of insurance, property ownership, business relationships, creditors' rights, and bankruptcy.

General Considerations

The legal rules protecting assets from judgment or bankruptcy creditors vary from state to state and differ under federal or state law. An appropriate program must address the applicable law in a particular state, personal factors, and various special circumstances. The program should be part of an integrated financial plan, covering the entire range of an individual's assets, and must not be exclusively "malpractice-driven."

Most importantly, planning and implementation must occur well in advance of any specific creditor problems to avoid allegations of fraudulent transfer and possible return of assets to the reach of creditors or to the bankruptcy estate. Property transfers should be based on reasons other than simply protection from creditors, and adequate records of all transactions should be maintained. Further considerations should include such unexpected events as possible future deterioration of family relationships (for example, divorce) and the potential personal liabilities of the "safe spouse," who may actually be vulnerable through professional or business activities, membership on boards of directors, or participation in a variety of organizations.

It must be emphasized that there is no single correct method, no uniform "generic" plan for asset protection. Each program is necessarily unique and should be based on an overall financial plan formulated with competent professional advice. The plan should integrate insolvency planning with other considerations, including insurance, tax planning, estate planning, and gifts to a spouse or children.

Common Misconceptions

Several commonly held erroneous beliefs are worthy of specific mention. The short discussions of each topic are designed to present a brief overview of problems and possibilities for asset protection, as a basis for further discussion with appropriate advisors.

1. **Not carrying liability insurance ("going bare") will prevent lawsuits**

    There is no objective basis for this belief. Should a lawsuit occur, the absence of insurance would require substantial personal expenses for defense costs, while personal and business assets can certainly be reached by creditors. Additionally, the risk of underinsurance is also substantial. Although it is widely believed that carrying low levels of insurance may reduce claim fre-

V / Claims Management

quency or claim severity, this has not been established by objective data. It is also possible that lack of liability insurance may jeopardize a discharge in bankruptcy if sufficient funds to pay malpractice judgment creditors are not available.

2. Carrying an "adequate" amount of liability insurance will prevent possible personal liability

This concept is false, since multimillion-dollar verdicts and awards are increasingly common, resulting in potential liability in excess of insurance coverage. The risks of a judgment above one's insurance limits are reduced, but not avoided, by adequate insurance coverage.

3. Jointly titled assets are protected from the creditors of one owner

This is a false assumption. Assets owned separately by one spouse are not reachable by creditors of the other spouse, and assets owned separately by children, as under Gifts to Minors or Transfers to Minors Acts, are not reachable except by the children's creditors. Joint ownership, however, subjects these assets to creditor claims, except in states permitting the protection of tenancy by the entirety between spouses, and litigation may result for the determination of the individual interests. Examples of jointly held property subject to claims against one owner include joint bank accounts, certificates of deposit, money market or mutual funds, savings accounts, brokerage accounts, joint accounts with children, and nonexempt real estate.

4. Organizing as a corporation protects individuals from personal liability

This is only partially true. The corporate structure does result in limitation of liability for shareholders. Individuals, however, remain personally liable for their own acts, as well as vicariously for the acts of others in certain circumstances. Corporate shareholders may be personally liable if improprieties in corporate organization or function permit a court to "pierce the corporate veil," thus removing the protection of the corporate structure. The corporate entity itself is subject to liability for its conduct and for the acts of its employees.

5. **Assets may be rendered judgment-proof from creditors, while still maintaining control and enjoyment of the assets**

    This assumption is false. Protective transfers can remove assets from the reach of creditors, and enjoyment of such assets may still be possible, but any degree of retained control over assets will probably permit creditors to reach them. The fundamentals of asset protection can be axiomatically stated as "Do it early—give up control."

    Creative management, which changes ownership and relinquishes control of assets, includes gifts to the spouse or children and the establishment of trusts which give control of assets to a trustee who administers the interests of the beneficiaries. Effective gifts, of course, are irrevocable. Trusts must be irrevocable to be effective for the protection of assets, but may be short-term, permitting asset reversion to the grantor after a period of years.

6. **Retirement assets, including ERISA-qualified or other plans, such as corporate pension plans, deferred compensation plans, KEOGH plans, or individual retirement accounts (IRAs), cannot be reached by creditors**

    This assumption may or may not be true, depending on state laws, federal law, court decisions, and other factors, which result in variable and incomplete protection for retirement plans.

7. **Bankruptcy is a fairly simple process that permits a fresh start**

    While bankruptcy may be a valid consideration in the event of a judgment in excess of insurance and property owned, the process should not be considered simple. A fresh start does result, but the final outcome will probably impact significantly on ones's lifestyle, through direct effects on assets and indirect effects on personal and business relationships, as well as credit ratings.

Conclusions

Adequate and timely planning for the protection of assets from possible future creditors, sometimes termed insolvency planning, can substantially reduce the risk of loss. The implementation of such a program requires advice from competent professionals knowledgeable in the laws of the particular state, detailed individualized considerations, and integration of general financial, tax, and estate planning. Asset transfer must occur well before the threatened claim, suit, or bankruptcy and must avoid circumstances permitting challenge on the basis of fraud upon creditors.

References

1. Halley MM, Fowks RJ, Bigler FC, Ryan DL (eds): *Medical Malpractice Solutions: Systems and Proposals for Injury Compensation.* Springfield, IL: Charles C Thomas, 1989.

2. Danner D: *Medical Malpractice: A Primer for Physicians.* Rochester, NY: The Lawyers Co-operative Publishing Co, 1988.

3. Spencer FC: The expert witness: One surgeon's opinion. *Bull Am Coll Surg,* 73(5):11-14; 43, 1988.

4. Rovit RL, Hauber C: The expert witness: Some observations and a response from neurosurgeons. *Bull Am Coll Surg,* 74(7):10-16, 1989.

5. Professional Liability Committee of the American College of Surgeons: Statement on the physician expert witness. *Bull Am Coll Surg,* 74(8):6-7, 1989.

Bibliography

American College of Obstetricians and Gynecologists: *Litigation Assistant: A Guide for the Defendant Physician.* Washington, DC: American College of Obstetricians and Gynecologists, 1987. [Reprinted in *Bull Am Coll Surg,* 72(5):26-44, 1987.]

Bankruptcy, *Corpus Juris Secundum.* St. Paul, MN: West Publishing Co, 1988.

Haydock RS, Herr DF, Stempel JW: *Fundamentals of Pretrial Litigation.* St. Paul, MN: West Publishing Co, 1985.

PROFESSIONAL LIABILITY/RISK MANAGEMENT – A MANUAL FOR SURGEONS

Hokanson D, Stevens J Jr, Koesten S, Schmidt RN, Woods R, Kirkland R, Meyer J: Protecting your assets from lawsuits. Seminar sponsored by Shook, Hardy & Bacon and Creative Planning, Inc, Kansas City, MO, October 1989.

Jury Verdict Research, Inc, 30700 Bainbridge Rd, Solon, OH: Personal communication.

Malpractice: Can you really protect your assets? In *Medical Economics for Surgeons*, pp 92-100, November 1989.

Penrod J: How to protect your assets. Postgraduate Course, Professional Liability/Risk Management/Legal Preparedness, American College of Surgeons, 76th Annual Clinical Congress, San Francisco, October 1990.

Perdo JR Jr, Borders JR: Legal criteria relating to individual protection of assets in the context of an increasing liability crisis. Postgraduate Course, Professional Liability/Risk Management/ Legal Preparedness, American College of Surgeons, 75th Annual Clinical Congress, Atlanta, October 1989.

11 United States Code (USC) 100 *et seq.*

VI / THE PSYCHOLOGICAL TRAUMA OF A MEDICAL MALPRACTICE SUIT: A PRACTICAL GUIDE

Editor's Note

Surgeons who are named in medical malpractice suits frequently experience a great deal of stress. This chapter discusses the wide range of emotions that are commonly observed in surgeons who are faced with the trauma of being sued.

The emotional or physical symptoms the surgeon can expect to experience are outlined for each step of the process—from the time of the initial complaint, during the period of litigation, and after the suit has been resolved. Methods for coping with the psychological trauma that is associated with each phase of a medical malpractice suit are described in detail.

The need to obtain social support, maintain self-esteem, and master the content of the case are explained as being important factors in dealing with the first phase of this stressful experience. Moreover, an explanation is provided as to why sharing concerns with family and friends, attempting to be patient through the course of this frustrating ordeal, and maintaining control of the daily work schedule are essential in minimizing anxiety during the resolution process.

It is pointed out that the surgeon should realize that some change in his or her practice pattern is a common occurrence following completion of the suit. The importance of seeking professional support when indicated is emphasized, particularly for the defendant surgeon who loses the case.

A surgeon may practice the highest level of competence in a surgical specialty, implement the latest directives in risk management strategies, and still be named in a medical malpractice suit. Our research has shown that the overwhelming majority of sued physicians experience some emotional disequilibrium as a result of being named and that the degree of symptomatology experienced is not related either to the merits or to the outcome of the suit.

Physicians expect and are accustomed to a high level of stress in their work. If there is a lack of challenge or stress in work, boredom and ineffectiveness can result. If, however, there is too much stress, an individual's ability to function optimally can be markedly compromised. Being named in a medical malpractice suit may generate such an overwhelming degree of added stress for doctors, that symptoms may develop, affecting every aspect of their personal and professional lives.

The Complaint

For many physicians, the incident of a complication or unanticipated poor outcome that eventually results in the filing of a medical malpractice suit has already been a source of soul searching and apprehension. The formal complaint often just substantiates the physician's worst fears—that the incident will someday lead to court where his or her decisions and behavior will have to be defended.

Every malpractice suit is unique. Each physician responds in his or her own way. Even if you have had more than one suit filed against you, each one is still unique. For most physicians, having had a previous experience of litigation does not prevent them from having the hurt feelings and/or the emotional disequilibrium that ensues. It does, however, often enable them to gain control and cope effectively with the situation more rapidly.

What Can I Expect?

Expect to have an *immediate* reaction. Often, it is a feeling of being stunned, feeling misunderstood, becoming immobilized, or being driven to frantic activity. This first reaction almost immediately is followed by intense feelings of anger and rage. Most physicians feel strongly that the charges filed against them are inappropriate and unjust, and they feel the need to communicate their feelings to someone. The complaint usually charges that the doctor has *failed* to provide the appropriate level of competent and professional care to the patient. It is this *accusation* that results in the feelings of hurt and narcissistic injury so often described by physicians as "devastating." These are *normal* reactions to a major assault on one's sense of self and personal integrity.

Also expect a lengthy process. Do not anticipate a speedy deliverance from this situation. Litigation often takes many years to resolve.

What Can I Do?

First, contact your insurer and follow directives. Too many physicians are driven to undertake activities, such as trying to talk with the aggrieved patient, that run counter to their best interests. You must understand that the legal system, into which you are now reluctantly drawn, does not function in the same manner as the medical environment. Follow the prescriptions of those who are familiar with the legal environment and processes.

Inquire about the average length of litigation in your own jurisdiction. In some areas, it may take five, seven, or even more years before a case may go to trial. Knowing that from the outset will enable you to plan and adapt more effectively.

Legal and insurance counsel will request that you do not talk to anyone about the details of your case, especially other physicians. Their fear is that a physician with whom you have talked in confidence may be called as an expert and compromise the defense of your case. Physicians, however, are human and therefore experience human reactions to any major life event, which litigation surely is. The single most critical need at such times is for social support. For their own psychological equilibrium, doctors need to talk with others; this human interaction will, in turn, enable them to function as good defendants. While remaining cognizant of the concerns of legal counsel, physicians should share their feelings about being sued with those among family and associates whom they feel will be most understanding of their present situation.

Once litigation has been set into motion, you can no longer prevent it from happening or alter the litigation process. This process makes many doctors feel a lack of control over subsequent events, resulting in feelings of uneasiness and vulnerability. This central feeling needs to be recognized and addressed.

Three major areas of intervention, however, will aid you in coping successfully with litigation. You can begin at once to devise and implement responses that best contribute to restoring equilibrium in your own life, including social support, enhancement of self-esteem and personal mastery, and changing the meaning of the event.

Social Support You should discuss your feelings about the event with whomever you feel most comfortable, such as your spouse, some peers, staff members, family members, or associates. Empathic responses by those with whom we associate are enormously supportive and restorative.

Self-esteem and Personal Mastery Litigation challenges our feelings of control over our lives. Often the allegation charges that we did not exert sufficient, or even absolute, control over the event in question, when at best only partial control could have been exerted. Since most physicians are cognizant that they have limited control over life and that they struggle daily with this knowledge, such a charge generates considerable anxiety and conflict.

In addition, physicians are accustomed to exerting control in their own medical environment. Being the object of a malpractice suit, however, demands that you submit yourself to a process over which you have little control or input. This procedure makes most physicians feel uneasy, leading to feelings of low self-esteem. You should, therefore, begin to evaluate your personal and professional lives and examine areas where you can exert increased control in order to counteract these feelings of lack of control. For example, if the organization of your office or the personnel who staff it are a source of frustration and conflict, you should use this opportunity to reorganize. Arrange your practice so that it is as manageable and anxiety free as possible. If you feel that your work is taking a toll on your personal and family life, this is the time to implement changes. The better you feel about your personal and work circumstances, the more effectively you will be able to defend yourself. The greater your feelings of control, the greater your feelings of self-esteem will be.

The accusation of having failed to perform competently is especially painful for highly trained and highly motivated physicians. Many times during the litigation process, your professional integrity will be challenged, resulting in feelings of doubt, shaken self-confidence, and low self-esteem. By mastering the content of the case, constantly working to improve your competence, studying, participating in professional activities, and maintaining some visibility with your peers, your self-esteem as a competent and caring physician can be greatly enhanced.

Most physicians are unfamiliar with the legal process. When sued for malpractice, many develop an attitude of disinterest until they are forced to be involved. A far better strategy is to prepare carefully for each interaction with the legal process. Prepare as though you were readying for your board examination. Leave nothing to chance! Remember, in your case, you are the expert—you were present at the time of the event in question.

Changing the Event's Meaning Similar to your reaction to any other event that occurs, you have to develop a way of conceptualizing and understanding litigation within the context of your life in order to develop some peace of mind and equilibrium about it. Despite a growing public understanding of the medical malpractice litigation problem as being an issue of compensation rather than an issue of competence, myths about the sued doctor remain. There is still a stigma associated with being sued that suggests that you are a "bad doctor." Despite public awareness of the fact that the practice of medicine is a human endeavor, and, therefore, mistakes and misjudgments can occur, people generally expect physicians to function "perfectly." The challenge to the sued physician is to live with this charge of negligence, which frequently is reinforced in depositions and through other legal maneuvers, while at the same time continuing to practice as a competent and caring physician. You can be successful in this regard only by changing your ideas and ways of thinking about the meaning of litigation. For many of us, making this change in our thinking involves the realization that good doctors who care for very sick or high-risk patients are most often the target of legal actions and that most malpractice suits eventually result in vindication for the physician.

During the Process

After the stunned feelings that result from the filing of the initial complaint have diminished, and the initial consultations with insurance and legal counsel have occurred, the physician is generally reassured and told to go back to work and "don't worry about it." Approaching the process of litigation with such lack of concern and equanimity, however, is not an easy task.

What Can I Expect?

Emotional or physical symptoms may develop. A period of emotional disequilibrium is extremely common following the initiation of a suit. Approximately 96 percent of all physicians we have studied acknowledged some symptoms for at least a limited period of time. The initial stressfulness of being served with a complaint is so overwhelming emotionally that doctors are not always immediately able to begin to initiate coping strategies, such as we described previously, that ordinarily would buffer the impact of the event. Our studies indicate that approximately 33 percent of physicians report, at some time during the process, a cluster of symptoms suggestive of major depressive disorder, characterized by depressed mood, insomnia, change in appetite, loss of interest in usual occupations, loss of energy, and similar other depressive symptoms. An average 26 percent of physicians develop a cluster of symptoms, suggestive of an adjustment disorder, characterized by pervasive anger, irritability, insomnia, frustration, inner tension, fatigue, or somatic symptoms. Approximately 16 percent of doctors develop a newly diagnosed or exacerbation of a previously diagnosed physical illness, such as hypertension, ulcer, or coronary artery disease. Any or all of these symptoms may be present throughout the entire process, but they occur most prominently when the physician has any interaction with the legal process, such as during deposition, hearings, or the trial.

Your spouse, family, staff, and associates will all be affected by your malpractice suit. Anything that affects you will necessarily affect your spouse, your marriage, and your children. If you develop insomnia, your spouse will be affected. If you begin to shun social interactions, the marriage may be strained. Your feelings of depression may lead to lack of interest in sexual activity. If you feel more preoccupied with your case when you are at home because your daily obligations provide a good distraction, your attention to and interest in your children may suffer. If you feel irritable and frustrated, your nurses, operating room personnel, and office staff may be subjected to your moods, leading to disruption in your work environment.

Medical work is often characterized by rapid decision-making in critical situations, with no time to research the literature or obtain a consultation. In the doctor's perception, legal work often appears to be a series of continuances and delaying maneuvers that give rise to frustration and anger.

Increasing discomfort and anxiety may arise about some areas of medical practice. Litigation often causes physicians to feel anxious in situations in which they feel a lack of control. Covering for associates when you are unfamiliar with their patients, covering the emergency room when you are expected to respond to all who seek assistance, performing certain procedures that are especially high risk, or working with patients who are at risk for complications or poor outcomes, particularly if they bear any resemblance to the subject of your litigation, may all cause you to feel anxious and uneasy.

What Can I Do?

Recognize the degree of disequilibrium you are currently experiencing. Physicians tend to use denial in their daily work lives. In other words, they either actively or unconsciously put out of their minds evidences of physical or psychological discomfort to the point that, to their way of thinking and, perhaps, for the moment, the source of discomfort does not even exist. To a degree, this is a necessary and useful mechanism that enables physicians to minimize their distractions and maximize their concentration. This use of denial, however, can be destructive if it is extended to the denial of physical symptoms, such as chest pain, insomnia, weight loss, depressed mood, or loss of interest in work or home life. If you are able to view your symptoms objectively or if symptoms of any significance persist, you should obtain appropriate medical and psychological consultations. Even when doctors obtain consultation, you should be cognizant of the fact that they often tend to minimize their complaints.

Particular attention should be paid to your interactions with family members, associates, and patients. Share your pain with your spouse. Our studies indicate that the doctor's spouse is the single greatest source of support for sued physicians. Most spouses are well able to understand the various difficulties of the process and want to participate in whatever way they can. In order to do so, however, they must *know* how you feel and what specific demands the lawsuit is making on you at a particular time.

The children should also be made aware of the problems you currently face. The amount of information that you and your spouse share with them is highly dependent on their age. Young children should be appropriately reassured and not burdened by the event; however, they should be brought to understand how difficult it is for the affected spouse. Episodes of irritability or frustration are not to be interpreted in personal terms, but rather should be explained such as, "Daddy is not really angry with you. He is upset about some problems at work." Older and adult children are often a source of considerable support for sued physicians.

Recognize that the legal process is characterized by cancellations, delays, and continuances. Doctors tend to become very frustrated and often fail to understand that the plaintiff's counsel wants you to be angry and disturbed. If, with your lawyer's help, you can understand that these delays are part of legal maneuvering, you can afford yourself more control. In general, the plaintiff's counsel wants you to settle the case. Deciding whether or not to settle is often an agonizing process for the defendant physician. Legal and insurance counsel must be considered, but your personal considerations and those of your spouse, family, and practice should also be carefully weighed. Do not ignore your spouse's input in making this important decision. Many physicians feel uneasy unless they have an opportunity for vindication at trial; others feel the need to dispose of the case as quickly as possible. Long-term consequences should be considered. Whether you settle or not is an individual decision to be made in each case.

Try to arrange your professional work so that it is under as much of your control as possible. During the period of litigation, you will, at least periodically, feel the anxiety and stress of being accused of having failed in some way to deliver competent and caring attention to your patient. There may, however, be situations in your work that accentuate these uncomfortable feelings. These situations may occur when working with patients who have particular medical conditions or certain personality characteristics, when dealing with specific procedures that are especially high risk, or when handling situations such as emergency room coverage or the supervision of house officers. You should carefully evaluate these situations and attempt to modify them, if at all possible, to diminish your work anxiety.

After the Litigation Is Resolved

Similar to so many other life events, when the litigation has been resolved, life goes on but is forever changed. Physicians agree that it is always better to win than to lose. In medical malpractice litigation, however, there are few winners, even when the judgment is in favor of the defendant. Most often, the doctor's feelings about career, work, patients, and self have been transformed by the experience.

What Can I Expect?

You can expect to have lingering feelings. Physicians who have won often find that they have pervasive feelings of injustice, of having wasted time and energy, and of having the desire to "get back at" the source of the problem. Many physicians talk of countersuit at such times. If you have lost, you find that you have persistent feelings of injured self-esteem, anger, and according to our studies, isolation and lack of support from within the medical community. For some physicians, symptoms persist; for others, new energy is unleashed.

What Can I Do?

You should recognize that there are common themes that preoccupy and, in some instances, plague physicians after the resolution of their case. These feelings include fears of additional suits, conflicts about control over one's work, rage at those who initiated or were exempted by the suit, and sadness over the loss.

After being involved in a lawsuit, physicians become phobic about certain patients, practice situations, or procedures. When confronted with the situation, the affected doctor becomes anxious and sometimes experiences somatic reactions. If this kind of reaction persists, consultation should be sought. Many physicians react by refusing to accept certain kinds of referrals or to perform certain procedures. If this approach works well in your situation and enables you to feel more comfortable, then you should follow it. If, however, your work demands that you participate in certain situations that are unusually anxiety-provoking, you should be realistic enough to assess whether your reactions in any way compromise patient care. If so, it is imperative that you seek consultation.

There will be conflicts about control over one's work. Physicians should arrange their work so that they feel that they are as much in control over it as possible. Otherwise, they may have increasing difficulty in making decisions, they may become easily distracted, and they may have impaired concentration.

Commonly, physicians express persistent anger at lawyers for initiating and profiting from malpractice suits. Many doctors feel that they are held to a higher standard than is any other group in society. This rage must be recognized, but should not be allowed to overwhelm and immobilize or embitter. It is far more effective to channel the energy generated by the anger into goal-directed activities, such as working with medical and specialty societies that are engaged in developing solutions to the problem.

One of the feelings most commonly expressed by physicians about their medical careers following the litigation experience is that "medicine isn't any fun anymore." There is no question that medical practice has changed and that involvement in a medical malpractice case changes both the doctor's self and manner of practice. An objective assessment of this reality, however, helps doctors to reinsert themselves into their work after the litigation experience. You should take whatever steps are necessary to enable you to practice the kind of medicine that you feel you can provide most effectively and to organize your life in a way that affords you sufficient gratification from both your personal and your professional lives.

If either physical or emotional symptoms persist, consultation should be obtained. If a physician has lost the suit, feelings often persist that need to be explored, particularly as they relate to plans for the future. Physician groups should attempt to address the lack of social support felt by doctors who have lost at trial or who have persistent feelings of loss secondary to the resolution of their case. These groups should be under the leadership of those who have had some experience with litigation.

After completion of the suit, many physicians use their new-found energy to develop new areas of competence in order to work with organized medical groups in addressing some of the issues facing medicine and to invest new energies into their family and social lives.

Conclusion

For most physicians, litigation is a stressful life experience; for a significant number, it is the most stressful experience of their lives. There are effective ways in which the stressfulness of the experience can be buffered. There are also ways to cope with it in a manner that contributes to personal and professional growth. Central to accomplishing these goals is an acceptance within the medical community of the reality that medical malpractice litigation is a rather common experience in a doctor's life. This acceptance should include the development of avenues of support and active interventions for physicians from within medical organizations. Developing this kind of interprofessional support will enable physicians to maintain their feelings of self-esteem and their energies in order to constantly improve their competence in delivering medical care that is of the highest possible quality to their patients.

GLOSSARY

abandonment
Termination of a physician-patient relationship without reasonable notice and without an opportunity for the patient to acquire adequate medical care, which results in some type of damage to the patient.

ad damnum clause
The part of a plaintiff's complaint that states the damages that are claimed.

admissible evidence
Evidence that may be properly introduced in a legal proceeding. The determination as to admissibility is based on legal rules of evidence and is made by the trial judge or a screening panel.

ADR
See *Alternative Dispute Resolution*.

affidavit
Voluntary, written statement of facts made under oath before an officer of the court or before a notary public.

agency
Relationship between persons in which one party authorizes the other to act for or represent that party.

allegation
Statement of a party to an action, made in a pleading, setting out what the party expects to prove.

alternative dispute resolution
Alternative dispute resolution, also called ADR, is a method or methods of resolving legal dispute outside the tort system.

answer
A legal document that contains a defendant's written response to a complaint or declaration in a legal proceeding. The answer typically either denies the allegations of the plaintiff or makes new allegations as to why the plaintiff should not recover.

appeal
The process by which a decision of a lower court is brought for review to a court of higher jurisdiction, typically known as an appellate court.

appellate court
The court that reviews trial court records. Appellate courts review the transcript of the trial court proceedings and determine whether there were errors of law committed by the trial court.

arbitration
The submission of a dispute to one or more neutral persons for a final and binding decision; usually displaces trial by judge and jury, but is based on the same substantive rules of law.

assault
Intentional and unauthorized act of placing another in apprehension of immediate bodily harm.

battery
The unauthorized and offensive touching of a person by another. In medical malpractice cases, battery is typically contact of some type with a patient who has not consented to the contact. Battery can be either a civil or a criminal offense.

Glossary

breach of contract
Failure, without legal excuse, to perform any promise which forms the whole or part of a contract.

breach of duty
Any violation or omission of a legal or moral duty.

burden of proof
The necessity or duty of affirmatively proving a fact or facts in dispute. The plaintiff typically has the burden of proof.

captain of the ship
A doctrine whereby the surgeon in charge of a medical team is liable for all the negligent acts of the members of the team.

captive insurance company
See *Insurance Company, Captive Insurance Company.*

carrier
An insurance company.

case
An action or cause of action; a matter in dispute; a lawsuit.

causation
Existence of a connection between the act or omission of the defendant and the injury suffered by the plaintiff. In a suit for negligence, the issue of causation usually requires proof that the plaintiff's harm resulted proximately from the negligence of the defendant.

certificate of merit
A tort reform mandated by law in several states that requires the plaintiff or his attorney in a medical malpractice case to file an affidavit or other sworn statement with (or shortly after) the complaint, stating that the case has been reviewed by a qualified expert who determined that, on its face, it is not frivolous.

circumstantial evidence
   See *Evidence, Circumstantial Evidence.*

claim
   In common parlance, any demand for compensation. What constitutes a claim that must be reported to an insurance company varies, but is always defined in the policy.

claims-made insurance policy
   Provides coverage for claims arising from incidents that both occur and are reported to the insurance company while the policy is continually in force. A claims-made policy is in force beginning with the starting date of the initial policy period and continues in force from that date through each subsequent renewal. When a claims-made policy is terminated, future claims arising from incidents that occurred during the policy period are not covered. See also *Tail Coverage.*

collateral sources rule
   A rule of law that prevents a court from subtracting from the damage award any payments that the plaintiff has received from other sources, such as workmen's compensation, health insurance, government benefits, or sick pay benefits.

common law
   That body of law that was passed down to the colonies by the British legal system and has been interpreted and refined by case law, as opposed to statutory law.

community standard rule
   See *Locality Rule.*

comparative negligence
   See *Negligence, Comparative Negligence.*

Glossary

compensable medical injuries
Defined medical injuries that would be compensated according to a schedule of benefits. Several tort reform proposals advocate an insurance mechanism that would remove medical malpractice cases from the court system into an administrative system that would compensate designated compensable events. See also *No-fault Compensation*.

compensation
Money payment for damages for the injury sustained proximately by a plaintiff caused by a defendant.

no-fault compensation
A method for compensating persons injured during the course of medical treatment, regardless of whether the injury was caused by the negligence or the fault of a health care provider.

compensation fund
See *Patient Compensation Fund*.

complaint
A legal document that is the initial pleading on the part of the plaintiff in a civil lawsuit. A complaint is sometimes known as a declaration. The purpose of this document is to give a defendant notice of the alleged facts constituting the cause of action. The complaint is usually attached to the summons.

confidentiality
The status of information transmitted during the course of a physician-patient relationship. The right of the patient to prevent disclosure of communications made between the patient and physician is also termed doctor-patient privilege. This privilege may not be recognized in all jurisdictions and may be limited in others.

consent
> Voluntary act by which one person agrees to allow another person to do something. "Express consent" is that directly and unequivocally given, either orally or in writing. "Implied consent" is that manifested by signs, actions, or facts or by inaction and silence, which raises a presumption that the consent has been given. It may be implied from conduct (implied-in-fact), for example, when someone rolls up his or her sleeve and extends his or her arm for vein puncture; or by the circumstance (implied-in-law), for example, in the case of an unconscious person in an emergency situation.

consultation
> Formal request by an attending physician of a medical specialist in a field for which information is sought. Ordinarily, a legal duty to consult arises when, after a reasonable length of time and effort on the part of the attending physician, the diagnosis is unusually difficult and uncertain, the therapy is ineffective, or the patient requests a consultation. To be legally sufficient, a consultation requires that the consultant personally examine the patient and the patient's records. A referral is to be distinguished from a consultation—a referral involves the transferral of the complete responsibility for the care of the patient to the specialist, whereas in a consultation, the attending physician retains primary responsibility.

contingency fee
> A fee agreement between the plaintiff and the plaintiff's attorney, whereby the plaintiff agrees to pay the attorney a percentage of the damages recovered.

contract
> Obligation that binds the involved parties to perform the terms of the agreement that they have reached, providing that there was a mutual meeting of the minds.

contributory negligence
See *Negligence, Contributory Negligence*.

court reporter
A professionally trained stenographer who transcribes deposition or trial testimony.

court trial
A trial without a jury, wherein a judge determines the facts as well as the law. Also called a bench trial.

damages
The sum of money a court or jury awards as compensation for a tort or breach of contract. The law recognizes certain categories of damages, including general, special, and punitive/exemplary damages.

general damages
Typically intangible damages, such as pain and suffering, disfigurement, interference with ordinary enjoyment of life, and loss of consortium (marital services).

punitive/exemplary damages
Damages awarded to the plaintiff in cases of intentional tort or gross negligence to punish the defendant or act as a deterrent to others.

special damages
Out-of-pocket damages that may be quantified, such as medical expenses, lost wages, and rehabilitation costs.

decedent
A dead person, usually the injured person, who would have been described as the plaintiff if still living.

defendant
The person against whom a civil or criminal action is brought.

defense attorney
The attorney who defends the person who is sued (defendant).

department
An organizational unit of the hospital or of the medical staff.

deposition
A discovery procedure whereby each party may question in person the other party or anyone who may possibly be a witness. Depositions are conducted before the trial under oath and are admissible at trial under certain circumstances.

directed verdict
Ruling by the trial judge that, as a matter of law, the verdict must be in favor of a particular party. A verdict is usually directed as a result of a clear failure to meet the burden of proof, sometimes referred to as a failure to establish a *prima facie* case. See also *Prima Facie Case*.

direction
Authoritative policy or procedural guidance for the accomplishment of a function or activity.

disability
Want of capability to perform an act. Incapacity for the full enjoyment of ordinary legal rights, actually because of a prior demonstrated impairment.

discovery
Pretrial procedures to learn of evidence in order to minimize the element of surprise at the time of trial. These typically include interrogatories and depositions, but can also include requests for admission of facts and requests for genuineness of documents.

discovery rule
A limitations statute does not begin to run until a patient knows or reasonably should know of an injury and also is aware, or reasonably should be aware, that the injury was wrongfully caused. See also *Period (Statute) of Repose* and *Statute of Limitations*.

dismissal
A legal denial. To dismiss a motion is to deny it; to dismiss an appeal is to affirm the judgment of the trial court.

doctor-patient privilege
See *Confidentiality*.

due care
Required degree of reasonable or ordinary observation and awareness that a person has and owes to another person by virtue of a special relationship or circumstance. Applicable as a standard of conduct in most personal injury cases, but not in medical malpractice cases, where the standard is that of a reasonable, qualified physician practicing the same specialty as the defendant.

duty
An obligation recognized by the law. A physician's duty to a patient is to provide the degree of care ordinarily exercised by physicians practicing in the same community or area of specialization.

evaluation
The review and assessment of the quality and appropriateness of an important aspect of care. The review and assessment is designed to identify problems and/or opportunities to improve care and, when they exist, to develop plans to solve the problems or take the opportunities to improve care.

evidence
All the means by which any alleged matter of fact, the truth of which is submitted to investigation at trial, is established or disproved. Evidence includes the testimony of witnesses, introduction of records, documents, exhibits, objects, or any other probative matter offered for the purpose of inducing belief in the party's contention by the judge or jury.

evidence *(continued)*

circumstantial evidence
Facts or circumstances that indirectly imply that the principal facts at issue actually occurred.

prima facie *evidence*
Evidence good and sufficient on its face.

experience rating
The practice of basing insurance premiums on past loss history.

expert opinion
The testimony of a person who has special training, knowledge, skill, or experience in an area relevant to resolution of the legal dispute.

expert witness
Person who has special training, knowledge, skill, or experience in an area relevant to resolution of the legal dispute, that is beyond the average person's knowledge, and who is allowed to offer an opinion as testimony in court.

federal court
Federal courts are another system of trial and appellate courts and, like state courts, only accept certain types of cases. Malpractice cases generally are not filed in the federal courts unless a patient is from one state and the health care provider from another state.

fiduciary
Person in a position of confidence or trust who undertakes a duty to act for the benefit of another under a given set of circumstances.

fraud
Intentionally misleading another person in a manner that causes legal injury to that person.

frequency of claims
> Refers to the number of claims that are filed. Frequency and average severity of claims are the fundamental variables used in determining insurance premiums. See also *Severity of Claims*.

future earnings
> Element of damages involving the specific "loss" of earnings that would probably have been made during a given future time had it not been for the injury that is the basis of the lawsuit.

general damages
> See *Damages, General Damages*.

Good Samaritan statute
> Statute enacted to encourage individuals to stop and assist victims of accidents by granting immunity from liability for any negligence resulting from attempts to give such emergency aid, without the expectation of payment.

guaranty fund
> Established by law in every state, this fund is typically maintained by the state commissioner of insurance to protect policyholders in the event that their insurer becomes insolvent or otherwise unable to meet its financial obligations. The fund is usually financed by an assessment against all property and casualty insurers regulated by the state.

guardian
> Person appointed by a court to manage the affairs of and to protect the interests of another who is adjudged incompetent by reason of age or physical or mental status and is thereby unable to manage his or her own affairs.

house staff
> Individuals, licensed as appropriate, who are graduates of medical, dental, osteopathic, or podiatric schools; who are appointed to a hospital professional graduate training program that is approved by a nationally recognized accrediting body approved by the commissioner of education; and who participate in patient care under the direction of licensed practitioners of the pertinent clinical disciplines who have clinical privileges in the hospital and are members of, or affiliated with, the medical staff.

hypothetical question
> A form of question put to a witness (usually an expert witness, but also a defendant or plaintiff) in which things which counsel claims are or will be proved are stated as a factual supposition, and the witness is asked to respond, state, or explain the conclusion based on the assumptions and question.

immunity
> In civil law, protection given certain individuals (personal immunity) or groups (institutional immunity) that may shield them from liability for certain acts or legal relationships. Ordinarily, the individual may still be sued, because immunity can be raised only as an affirmative defense to the complaint, that is, after a lawsuit has been filed.

impairment
> Measurable dysfunction of a person.

important aspect of care
> Clinical activities that involve a high volume of patients, entail a high degree of risk for patients, and/or tend to produce problems for staff or patients. Such activities are deemed most important for purposes of monitoring and evaluation.

Glossary

incapacity
> Inability and preclusion of exercising an inherent right or carrying out a transaction because of a legal impediment or impairment.

incident report
> A written report by either a patient or a staff member that documents any unusual problem, incident, or other situation for which a patient or staff member wishes to have follow-up action taken by appropriate administrative or supervisory personnel.

indemnity
> Agreement whereby a party guarantees reimbursement for possible losses.

indicator
> A defined, measurable variable used to monitor the quality or appropriateness of an important aspect of patient care. Indicators can be activities, events, occurrences, or outcomes for which data should be collected to allow comparison with the threshold for evaluation related to each indicator. Indicators are often guidelines for care or practice that include objective clinical criteria based on authoritative sources, such as the clinical literature and consensus panels.

informed consent
> A legal doctrine that requires a physician to obtain consent for treatment rendered or an operation performed; without an informed consent, the physician may be held liable for violation of the patient's rights, regardless of whether the treatment was appropriate and rendered with due care. See also *Battery*.

insurance
> Written agreement (the insurance policy) wherein, for premium payments, the insurance company (the insurer) promises to compensate the policy holder (the insured) for losses which occur as defined in the agreement.

insurance company
> A company, also known as a provider or a carrier, that is licensed by a state to sell some or all types of insurance.
>
> ***captive insurance company***
>> An alternative insurance mechanism in which a corporation, hospital, or group of such entities form their own insurance company. These captives are typically capitalized by their parent(s), are professionally managed, and issue insurance policies modeled after those used in the commercial market. These insurance policies are issued to risks that include, but are not limited to, the founding parents. Captives are typically located off-shore and have favorable tax and regulatory treatment compared with those of domestic insurers.

intent
> Voluntary function of a person's mind in purposely performing a perceivable act.

interrogatories
> A discovery procedure in which one party submits a series of written questions to the opposing party, who must answer in writing under oath within a certain period of time. The answers are admissible at trial under certain circumstances.

joint and several liability
> A legal doctrine whereby each individual defendant is responsible for the entire amount of damages awarded against all defendants.

joint underwriting association
> A government-administered risk pooling arrangement, commonly referred to as a JUA, established by law in a number of states to provide professional liability insurance to health care providers. A JUA is structured to be financed by assessments against its participants, but typically also has the authority to assess property and casualty insurers licensed to do business in the state in the event of a deficit.

JUA
See *Joint Underwriting Association*.

judgment
The final entry in the record of a case, which is binding upon the parties unless it is overturned or modified on appeal. A judgment typically consists of a finding in favor of one or more of the parties and an assessment of damages and costs.

jury
Certain number of persons selected according to law, sworn to inquire of certain matters of fact and declare the truth upon evidence to be laid before them. In trying issues of fact, they function under supervision of a judge who is empowered to instruct them on the law. Their verdict may be set aside if, in the judge's opinion, it is contrary to law or evidence.

jury trial
A trial in which six to 12 registered voters are impaneled to hear the evidence, determine the facts, and render a verdict. In most states, the verdict must be unanimous.

law
Documented guide to conduct, based on the expression of how society views the responsibility of each individual to other individuals. It includes an amalgam of principles that provide a basis for dispute resolution, in addition to the ultimate resolution itself, if necessary.

lawsuit
Civil legal action or adversarial proceeding by which a plaintiff seeks enforcement of his or her rights or redress for the transgression of them by a defendant.

liability
> Obligation that a person has incurred or might incur through any act or omission. In civil matters, liability for damages is for a definite amount, ascertained by a final judgment based on the preponderance of the evidence that demonstrates that the defendant was responsible for the plaintiff's injury and, therefore, is obligated to provide compensation to the plaintiff.

license
> Permit from an appropriate governmental agency, allowing certain acts to be performed, usually for a specific period of time.

limits of coverage
> The maximum amount an insured or a claimant can collect under the terms of a policy. Professional liability policies typically specify limits per claim and a cumulative limit for all claims incurred during the term of a contract, for example, $1 million (per claim)/$3 million (per term).

litigation
> Trial of a dispute in a court of law to determine factual and legal issues, rights, and duties between the parties to the controversy.

locality rule
> The test historically used by courts to determine the standard of care owed by health care providers to patients. The rule holds that health care providers have the duty to render care consistent with the care of other competent or prudent practitioners under the same or similar circumstances in the same or similar community. Most states have displaced the locality rule with the requirement that care must be consistent with national standards. See also *Standard of Care*.

Glossary

loss of consortium
A claim for damages by the spouse of an injured party for the loss of care, comfort, society, and interference with sexual relations. See also *Damages, General Damages.*

malpractice
Professional negligence. In medical terms, it is the failure to exercise that degree of care as is used by reasonably careful physicians, in the same or similar circumstances, of like qualifications. The failure to meet this acceptable standard of care must cause the patient injury.

matter of law
Point that must be decided on the basis of either applicable statute or decisions of case law.

matter of record
Any judicial matter or proceeding entered on the records of a court and to be proved by production of such records.

mediation
The submission of a dispute to an outside facilitator, often with specialized expertise, for assistance in reaching a mutually acceptable settlement. The procedure is private, voluntary, and nonbinding.

minor
Person who has not yet reached the statutorily determined age of legal transactional capacity. As a result of this presumed legal incompetence, minors ordinarily cannot consent to their own medical treatment unless they are "emancipated," that is, substantially independent from their parents, supporting themselves, married, or otherwise on their own, or unless a statute provides otherwise.

misrepresentation

Manifestation by words or other conduct by one person to another which, under the circumstances, amounts to an assertion not in accordance with the facts. An incorrect or false representation of a condition other and different from that which exists. A "fraudulent misrepresentation" is made by a person with a knowledge of the falsity of the representation, which causes the other party to enter into an arrangement or an agreement. A "negligent misrepresentation" is made by a person who has no reasonable grounds for believing that the representation is true, even though he does not know that it is untrue, or even believes it to be true. An "innocent misrepresentation" is made by a person who had reasonable grounds for believing that the representation was true.

monitoring

The systematic and ongoing collection and organization of data related to the indicators of the quality and appropriateness of important aspects of care and the comparison of the level of performance with thresholds for evaluation to determine the need for evaluation.

motion

Written or oral court plea requesting that a judge make an order or ruling affecting the lawsuit.

negligence

Legal cause of action involving the failure to exercise the degree of diligence and care that a reasonably and ordinarily prudent person would exercise under the same or similar circumstances, and the result of which is the breach of a legal duty, which proximately causes an injury which the law recognizes as deserving of compensation. The standard of care of a defendant physician in a medical malpractice case is not that of the reasonable and ordinarily prudent person (such as an automobile operator), but rather, that of the reasonably qualified physician practicing in the same area of specialization or general practice as that of the defendant physician.

comparative negligence
An affirmative defense that compares the negligence of the defendant to that of the plaintiff. The plaintiff may recover damages from a negligent defendant even if the plaintiff and defendant are equally at fault. The plaintiff's damages are reduced, however, by the percentage that his or her own fault contributed to the overall damage.

contributory negligence
An affirmative defense that prevents recovery against a defendant when the plaintiff's own negligence contributed to his or her own injury, even though the defendant's negligence may also have contributed to the injury.

no-fault compensation
See *Compensation, No-fault Compensation*.

occurrence policy
A type of policy in which the policyholder is covered for any incident that occurs during the term of the policy, regardless of when a claim arising from the incident is made. Occurrence policies have been largely supplanted by "claims-made" coverage in the medical liability insurance market. See also *Claims-made Insurance Policy*.

pain and suffering
Element of "compensatory" nonpecuniary damages that allows recovery for the mental anguish and/or physical pain endured by the plaintiff as a result of injury for which the plaintiff seeks redress. See also *Damages, General Damages*.

partnership
: Contractual state resulting from the agreement of two or more associates (partners) to engage in a commercial enterprise for the benefit of all co-partners, and to share the profits and losses proportionally. Each person acts as a principal as well as an agent for his co-partners. Thus, where losses occur, each partner is personally responsible for the payment of all partnership debts.

patient compensation fund
: A fund established by law in some states that pays benefits to patients injured in the course of medical treatment. Benefits may be awarded on either a fault basis or a no-fault basis, depending on the state program. The fund's benefits may either supplement the payment made by a defendant in a medical malpractice claim or be the primary compensation, again depending on the state program.

periodic payments
: Damages paid to a plaintiff over a period of time instead of in a lump sum all at once. If a state law permits, periodic payments may be ordered when the damages exceed a certain amount.

period (statute) of repose
: A limit on the time within which a suit may be brought, with the limit defined from the date of the defendant's alleged harmful act, as opposed to the date the plaintiff discovered the injury. See also *Discovery Rule* and *Statute of Limitations*.

perjury
: Willful giving of false testimony under oath.

plaintiff
: Party who files or initiates a civil lawsuit, seeking relief or compensation for damages or other legal relief.

Glossary

pleading
Legal documents filed in a lawsuit, which identify and clarify the issues in dispute; includes the plaintiff's complaint and the defendant's answer.

policy
The contractual agreement between an insurance company and its insured. The policy sets forth the rights and obligations of both parties to the agreement.

possibility
A less than probable chance without excluding the idea of feasibility. A less than 50 percent chance that something occurred.

premium
The amount of money an insured pays for an insurance policy. The premium is calculated by the insurance company's underwriters to bring in enough money to establish reserves for future losses, pay current losses, cover the company's operating expenses, including the cost of defending claims, and generate a profit if the company is organized as a profit-making business. See *Underwriting*.

pretrial screening
A tort reform established in a number of states to require or encourage plaintiffs to participate in a procedure for determining if the claim is unfounded or has merit prior to pursuing litigation in the courts. States differ in the structure of the pretrial screening process, the type of evidence that will be reviewed, and in the rules regarding whether the pretrial screening conclusion is admissible as evidence in subsequent litigation.

prima facie
On the first appearance.

prima facie *case*
A complaint that apparently contains all the necessary legal elements for a recognized cause of action and will suffice until contradicted and overcome by other evidence.

probability
Reasonable ground of presumption because there is more evidence in favor of the existence of a given proposition than there is against it; more likely than not; 50.1 percent; but not a possibility.

proximate cause
See *Causation*.

publication
Oral or written act that makes defamatory material available to persons other than the person defamed.

punitive/exemplary damages
See *Damages, Punitive/Exemplary Damages*.

qualifications
The credentials or presumed capability of a professional to perform a task.

quality assurance
Process to ensure appropriateness and adequacy in the care of patients.

rate
An insurance term, reflecting the basis or classification upon which the premium is based; often used as a synonym for premium. See also *Premium*.

reasonable
Fit and appropriate to the end in view, not immoderate or excessive.

Glossary

reasonable degree of medical certainty
As used in personal injury lawsuits, a term implying more than mere conjecture, possibility, consistent with or speculative; similar to a probability, more likely than not, 50.1 percent, but an overwhelming likelihood or scientific certainty is not required.

release
Statement signed by a person relinquishing a right or claim against another person or persons usually for a payment or other valuable consideration. The intent is that the person's alleged injury has been fully satisfied. It is to be distinguished from a covenant not to sue, which is a partial release by the plaintiff, involving the plaintiff's giving up of the plaintiff's claim against one defendant for money damages, but not giving up the plaintiff's claim against other defendants.

reporting requirement
The contractual obligation of the insured to promptly report to the carrier any claim for damages that is or may be asserted against the insured. What constitutes a claim that must be reported varies from company to company, but is always defined in the policy.

reserve
Money set aside and invested by insurance companies to pay estimated future losses. A company's claims department typically specifies a reserve amount for every claim that is filed, which may be modified as the claim proceeds in the courts.

res ipsa loquitur
"The thing speaks for itself." A case in which the personal injuries and/or property damage would not have occurred in the absence of negligence. In medical malpractice cases, it allows a patient to prove his or her case without the necessity of an expert witness to testify that the defendant physician violated the standards of care. It is applicable only in those instances in which negli-

gence is clear and obvious, even to a layman, such as foreign object cases in which a surgeon leaves a sponge in the patient following surgical operation.

respondeat superior
"Let the master answer." The legal principle that makes an employer liable for civil wrongs committed by employees within the course and scope of their employment.

rights
Power or demands, inherent in one person, which that person is entitled to have, or to do, or to receive from others within the prescribed limits of the law.

risk
The chance of loss. The uncertainty that exists as to actual occurrence of loss caused by some event or happening. "Pure risk" is uncertainty as to whether loss will occur. In "speculative risk," there is uncertainty about an event that could produce loss. Pure risk is insurable; speculative risk usually is not.

risk management
A systematic approach to identifying, evaluating, reducing, or eliminating risk due to an undesirable deviation from an anticipated outcome, thereby preventing the loss of financial assets resulting from injury to patients.

risk retention group
A group of similarly situated persons or entities that are permitted under federal law to organize across state lines for the purpose of pooling their liability risk and self-insuring. If the group is licensed in one state, it is permitted to solicit business and sell insurance nationwide, without fulfilling each state's licensure requirements.

settlement
An agreement made between the parties to a lawsuit or a claim which resolves their legal dispute.

structured settlement
Settlement agreement between the parties to a lawsuit or a claim in which the damages are paid to the plaintiff over a period of time instead of in a lump sum all at once. These settlements are usually financed through the purchase of an annuity.

severity of claims
Also known as claim magnitude, this is the dollar value of a claim as determined by jury verdict or settlement agreement. Claim frequency and average severity are the principal variables used in determining insurance premiums. See also *Frequency of Claims*.

special damages
See *Damages, Special Damages*.

standard of care
A term used in the legal definition of medical malpractice. A physician is required to adhere to the standards of practice of reasonably competent physicians, in the same or similar circumstances, with comparable training and experience.

stare decisis
A legal judgment based upon a previous decision.

statute of repose
See *Period (Statute) of Repose*.

statutes of limitation
The time period set forth by statute in which a plaintiff may file a lawsuit. Once this period expires, the plaintiff's lawsuit is barred if the defendant asserts the affirmative defense of the statute of limitations.

stipulation

An agreement made by both parties to the litigation regulating any matter related to the case, proceeding, or trial. For instance, litigants can agree to extend the time period for pleadings or to admit certain facts into evidence at trial.

structured settlement

See *Settlement, Structured Settlement*.

subpoena

Court order requiring a witness to appear at a certain proceeding to give testimony or produce documents.

suit

See *Lawsuit*.

summary judgment

Granting of a judgment in favor of either party prior to trial. Summary judgment is only granted when there is no factual dispute, and one of the parties is entitled to judgment as a matter of law.

summons

A legal document which is attached to the complaint or declaration in a lawsuit. It orders the defendant or the defendant's attorney to file an answer within a specified period of time.

tail coverage

Tail coverage, the common term for extended reporting endorsement, is a supplemental policy obtained from a claims-made carrier to provide coverage for any incident that occurred while the claims-made insurance was in effect, but had not been brought as a claim by the time the insurer/policyholder relationship terminated. Tail coverage is generally needed at the time of death or retirement or upon the decision to change claims-made carrier.

Glossary

testimony
Oral evidence presented under oath during a judicial proceeding by a competent witness in order to prove a fact. Testimony is to be distinguished from nonoral types of proof, such as types of physical evidence (for example, documents).

therapeutic privilege
Withholding of information from a patient by a physician when knowledge of the information might be considered extremely injurious to the patient.

thresholds for evaluation
A preestablished level of performance related to an indicator at which further evaluation of the quality and appropriateness of an important aspect of care is initiated.

tort
A civil wrong, other than a breach of contract, for which the law provides a remedy in the form of monetary damages.

tort reform
A term used to collectively describe a number of legislative and judicial modifications to traditional tort law.

trial
Judicial examination, before a proper court having jurisdiction of issues of law or fact between the litigating parties in accordance with the governing law.

trial court
The court of first jurisdiction where the pleadings are filed, the witnesses appear, testimony is taken, and a judgment is entered; also referred to as the lower court.

underwriting
The process by which a company evaluates and classifies risks and measures and calculates the cost of protection, within the framework of the rules, rates, and coverage forms that are permitted by law in a particular state.

unit
A functional division or facility of the hospital.

verdict
The formal decision or finding made by a jury or judge. The verdict is rendered in favor of the plaintiff or defendant, and damages are typically awarded when the verdict is in favor of the plaintiff.

vicarious liability
Civil liability for the torts of others. Physicians may be vicariously liable for the negligent acts of their employees committed within the scope of their employment. See also *Respondeat Superior*. In the hospital setting, a surgeon may be vicariously liable for the negligent acts of all members of the surgical team. See also *Captain of the Ship*.

witness
Person who is called to give testimony in a court of law.

written consent
Consent given in writing, specifically empowering someone to do something.

wrongful death
A type of lawsuit brought on behalf of a deceased person's estate that alleges that death was attributable to the willful or negligent act of another.

INDEX

Abandonment, 19–20, 114, 213
Abbreviations in medical records, 126
Abdominal pain malpractice case, 57–59
Abortion consent, 123
Accountability of residents and supervisors, 143–144
ACOG (American College of Obstetricians and Gynecologists), 6, 143
Acts of others, liability for, 47–54, 144n, 193
Ad damnum clause, 68, 213
Adenoids surgery malpractice case, 35–36
Ad Hoc Regental Committee on Professional Liability, 3–4
Adjustment disorder symptoms, 206
Administrative alternatives to dispute resolution, 75–79
Admissible evidence, 213
ADR (alternative dispute resolution), 75–87, 187, 189, 214
Adverse patient occurrences (events), 6, 126, 135, 139
Affidavits, 213
Agency relationship, 47–54, 144n, 213. See also Captain of the ship doctrine; *Respondeat superior* doctrine; Vicarious liability doctrine
Allegations, 213

Alternative dispute resolution (ADR), 75–87, 187, 189, 214
AMA/Specialty Society Medical Liability Project, 4, 75–79
American College of Obstetricians and Gynecologists (ACOG), 6, 143
American College of Surgeons activities, 3–6
American Law Institute, 87
American Medical Association, 4, 75–79, 148–150
Amputation malpractice case, 40–41
Anesthesia malpractice cases, 48–49, 51–53
Anesthesia risks in consent forms, 120, 121
Answers in legal proceedings, 214, 233. *See also* Questions, answering
Antibiotic malpractice case, 182–183
Antitrust liability immunity, 66
Apologizing for appointment delays, 111
Appeal process, 214
Appeals, dismissal of, 221
Appellate courts, 77, 78, 214
Appointments
  delays in, 110–111
  missed, 127, 130
  scheduling, 110–111
  time and frequency of, 114
Arbitration of disputes, 68, 75, 187, 189, 214

Aristotle, 11
Assaults, 214
Asset protection, 191–195
Associates, interactions with, 206–208
Attorneys
 anger at, 210–211
 conflict of interest of, 161
 defense, 168, 219
  junior, 160–161
  meetings with, 163, 164, 167
  more than one, value of, 161
  relationship with, 157–164, 176
  selecting, 160–161
  for self-insured surgeons, 158
  working with, 162–164
 during depositions, 165–166, 168–171
 fees of, 68–69, 80, 82, 218
 inquiries from, 131
 in lawsuit settlement, 188–189
 plaintiff, 165–166, 168–171
Audiovisual aids, 121–123
Authoritative textbook references, 171, 179

Baird v. Sickler, 51–52
Bankruptcy, 193, 194
Bankruptcy creditors, 191–192
Battery, 214
Bench (court) trials, 219
Bile duct obstruction malpractice case, 26–27
Billing procedures, 131
Birth-related neurologic injuries, 86
"Bladder" surgery malpractice case, 31–32
Blind settlement offers, 76
Blood urea nitrogen in malpractice case, 182–183
Borrowed servant doctrine, 50–54, 144n
Brain damage malpractice case, 41–42

Breach of
 contract, 44–47, 74, 215
 duty, 32–36, 215
 professional standards, 19–20
 warranty, 46
Breast surgery malpractice cases, 13, 43–44
Brittain, R. S., 125
Brochures as informational aid, 121–123
Burden of proof, 215
Burned hand malpractice case, 35–36
Bush v. United States, 24–27, 32
Butler v. Berkeley, 61–62

Cancer malpractice cases
 breast, 13, 43–44
 cervix, 23–24
 Hodgkin's disease, 55–56
 knee, 18
 lung, 41–42
 ovaries, 64–65
 pancreas, 24–26, 32
 rectal stump, 29–30
 urinary (squamous cell), 31–32
Captain of the ship doctrine, 51–54, 144n, 215
Captive insurance companies, 226
Cardiac surgery malpractice cases, 36–37, 181–183
Care. *See also* Health care *entries*
 continuing, instructions for, 148. *See also* Follow-up care
 dissatisfaction with, documenting, 131
 due, 221
 evaluation of, 221
 follow-up. *See* Follow-up care
 important aspects of, 224
 indicators of, 139–141, 225, 230, 239
 postoperative, in malpractice cases, 27–31
 by residents, in problem situations, 149
 standard of. *See* Standard of care

Index

Care *(continued)*
 surgeons showing, during trial, 173–174, 177
Carpal tunnel syndrome malpractice case, 53–54
Carriers. *See* Insurance companies
Cases. *See also* Lawsuits; Litigation; *specific entries, eg:* Cancer malpractice cases; Tooth extraction malpractice case
 defined, 215
 prima facie, defined, 234
Catheterization of vein malpractice case, 55–56
Causation in legal proceedings, 36–39, 215
Certificates of merit, 215
Cervical cancer malpractice case, 23–24
Chain of command in hospitals, 149
Channeling programs for insurance coverage, 98–99
Charitable immunity, 224
Chemically impaired surgeons, 149–150
Chief surgeons, liability of, 51–54
Child(ren). *See also* Minors, defined
 assets given to, 194
 assets owned by, 193
 damages awarded to, 40–42
 damages awarded to parents of, 40–42
 informed consent for, 123
 injured infant, compensation for, 86
 malpractice cases involving, 41–42, 48–49
 reassuring, 208
 in statutes of limitations, 60
 vaccine injuries of, 85–86
Cholecystitis malpractice case, 57–59
Circumstantial evidence, 35–36, 222

Civil lawsuits. *See* Lawsuits
Civil litigation, defined, 157. *See also* Lawsuits; Litigation
Claim magnitude, 237
Claims, 216
 frequency of, 223
 medical malpractice. *See* Medical malpractice claims
 severity of, 237
Claims–made insurance policies, 100–102, 216
 extended reporting endorsements (tail coverage) in, 100–102, 238
Claims management, 6, 157–195
 asset protection in, 191–195
 defined, 155
 lawsuit settlement in, 185–189
 surgeon-attorney relationship in, 157–164, 176
 trials in, 173–183
Clarity of communication in testimony, 178–179
Cleocin (clindamycin) malpractice case, 182–183
Clinical outcomes, poor, in medical records, 128
Clitoris excision malpractice case, 31–32
Code blue plans for office, 130
Code of Hammurabi, 11
Collateral sources rule, 69, 74–75, 80, 216
College of Physicians of London, 12
Committees in risk management and quality assurance, 135–136
Common bile duct obstruction malpractice case, 26–27
Common law, 11, 12, 216
Communication
 clarity of, in testimony, 178–179
 in coping with lawsuits, 203–204
 between physicians and patients, 66, 145–147, 217
 in quality assurance, 139–141

Communication *(continued)*
  between residents and patients, 145–147
  between residents and supervisors, 144–145
Communication skills, 132
Community standard (locality) rule, 21–22, 228
Comparative negligence, 15, 62–63, 71, 231
Compassion shown by surgeon during trial, 177
Compensable medical injuries, 81–82, 217
Compensation
  for damages, 39–42, 217, 219
  no-fault, 81–87, 99, 103, 217, 232
  deferred, 194
Compensatory damages, 39–42
Competence of surgeons in trials, 173, 177
Complaint in lawsuits, 157–159, 201–205, 217, 233
Complications, information about
  in consent form, 121
  in medical records, 128
  not wanted by patients, 116–117
  patients informed of, 146–147
Conciliation in dispute resolution, 189
Confidentiality in surgeon-patient relationship, 66, 217
Conflict of interest of attorneys, 161
Consent
  defined, 218
  express, 218
  implied, 218
  informed. *See* Informed consent
  in risk prevention, 115–124
  verbal, 119
  written, 240
Consent forms, 116–123
  drafting, 120–121
  hospital-preferred, 146
  information aids noted in, 122–123

medical society endorsement of, 120
  omnibus consent provision in, 121–122
  risks in, 121
  signatures in, 121
Consortium, loss of, 39–40, 82, 229
Consultations, 218
  after litigation, 210, 211
  during litigation, 208
  in medical records, 127
  with patients, 111–112
Contingency fees, 68–69, 82, 218
Continuing care, instructions for, 148
Continuing treatment in statutes of limitations, 71
Contract(s)
  breach of, 44–47, 74, 215
  defined, 218
  in dispute resolution, 79
  express, 44–47
  implied, 44–45
  pretreatment, 79
  private, 79
Contract liability, 44–47
Contributory negligence, 62, 63, 231
Control in coping with lawsuits, 204, 209, 210
Corporate organization and personal liability, 193
Countersuits, 74
Court-appointed neutral experts, 189
Court reporters, 219
Courtroom trials. *See* Trials
Courts
  appellate, 77, 78, 214
  federal, 222
  trial, 214, 239
Court (bench) trials, 219. *See also* Trials
Covenants not to sue, 235
Coverage in insurance, 191, 193, 228
Cranial nerve damage from surgery, 37

Index

Credibility of surgeons in trials, 174, 177–178
Creditors (in asset protection), 191–194
Criminal activity, reporting, 66
Criminal law versus tort law, 12
Crohn's disease malpractice case, 29–30
Cross v. Guthrey, 13
Cross-examination of expert witnesses, 181, 183

Damages
  ad damnum clause involving, 68, 213
  compensation for, 39–42, 217, 219
  no-fault, 81–87, 99, 103, 217, 232
  compensatory, 39–42
  defined, 219
  future earnings loss in, 223
  general (intangible), 82, 219
  liability for, 68, 71–72, 74, 75, 226
  in medical malpractice claims, 39–44
    awarded by hearing examiner, 76–77
    awarded by jury, 40–42, 63, 70–71, 191
    of comparative negligence, 62–63
    modifying, 72
    recovery of, 21–32
    sympathy or prejudice in, 41–42
  in tort reform, 68, 71–72, 74
  pain and suffering in, 231
  periodic payments of, 72, 75, 232
  punitive/exemplary, 39–40, 42–44, 72–73, 82, 219
  special (out-of-pocket), 219
Danner, D., 125, 170
Data
  collecting, 69, 137–140
  on indicators of care, monitoring, 230
  in medical records, studying, 162–163, 166, 169, 176
  processing and evaluating, 69
  in quality assurance, 138–140
Data banks, 69, 139, 186
Davis v. Weiskopf, 17–18
Death, wrongful, 240
Decedents, 219
Declaration (complaint) in lawsuits, 157–159, 201–205, 217, 233
"Deep pocket" theory, 48, 71. *See also* Vicarious liability doctrine
Defamatory material, 234
Defendants, 219
  surgeons as, 151–171, 173–183, 185–189, 199, 201–212. *See also* Trials, defendant in
Defense (in litigation), development of, 159
Defense attorneys. *See* Attorneys, defense
Defenses against malpractice claims, 54–66
  patient negligence, 61–63
  procedural, 57–63
  standard of care, 54–56
  statutes of limitations, 56–61
  statutory, 63–66
Deferred compensation plans, 194
Deformity of finger malpractice case, 46–47
Dehydration malpractice case, 182–183
Delays in litigation process, 208–209
Delinquent accounts, 131
Demeanor, professional, 167–168, 175–177
Denial mechanism during litigation, 207–208
Departments (units) of hospitals, 135–141, 149, 220, 240
Depositions, 162, 165–171
  attorneys in, 165–166, 168–171

245

Depositions *(continued)*
  defined, 165, 220
  demeanor during, 167–168
  emotional reactions during, 168
  by expert witnesses, 180
  materials related to, handling, 131
  preparing for, 166–167
  questions during, 167–171
  recesses during, 168
  statements in, trial usage of, 166
  textbook references during, 171
Depression during litigation, 206–207
Diagnosis
  optimal methods of, 83
  in standard of care, 22–26
  tentative, in medical records, 126–127
Diagnostic tests, 23–27, 29, 130, 132, 148
Directed verdicts, 220
Direction, defined, 220
Disability, defined, 220. *See also* Incapacity; Incompetent *entries*; Mentally disabled
Disaster plans for office, 130
Disciplinary action, immunity from, 66
Disclosure in informed consent, 115, 116, 122–123
Discovery, 76, 162, 220. *See also* Depositions; Interrogatories
Discovery rule, 57–61, 71, 220. *See also* Period of repose; Statutes of limitations
Dismissal of motions or appeals, 221
Disparaging remarks in medical records, 128
Disputes. *See specific entries, eg:* Alternative dispute resolution; Lawsuits; Mediation of disputes
Diverticulum of urethra malpractice case, 45–46

Doctor-patient privilege, 217. *See also* Surgeon-patient relationship
Documentation
  of consent. *See* Consent forms
  of follow-up care plans, 131–132
  for JCAHO accreditation, 140
  of medical emergencies without informed sent, 116
  in medical records, 125–128, 130, 149
  of patient dissatisfaction, 131
  of problematic care by residents, 149
  in risk prevention, 5, 6
Drugs. *See* Chemically impaired surgeons; Prescriptions
Due care standard, 221
Duty, 221
  breach of, 32–36, 215

Early offer and recovery system, 79–81
Earnings, future, loss of, 40–41, 223
Educational materials for patients, 122–123, 128
Emergencies and informed consent, 116
Emergency aid statutes, 63–65, 223
Emergency overruling of impaired surgeons, 150
Emergency plans for office, 130
Emotional disequilibrium during litigation, 206–208
Emotional reactions to medical malpractice claims, 202, 203
  during depositions, 168
  in litigation process, 206–207
  after resolution, 209–211
  during trial, 174, 176–177
Employer liability for employee actions, 48–50, 144n, 193, 236, 240
Employment agencies, 49
Employment relationship in agency law, 48–54, 144n, 236, 240

Index

Enterprise Responsibility for Personal Injury (American Law Institute), 87
ERISA-qualified retirement plans, 194
Ethical issues addressed by residents, 148–150
Evaluation (of care), 221
  thresholds for, 140–141, 239
Evidence
  admissible, 213
  circumstantial, 35–36, 222
  defined, 221
  preponderance of, 21
  prima facie, defined 222
Exemplary/punitive damages, 39–40, 42–44, 72–73, 82, 219
Experience ratings for insurance, 104, 222
Experimental therapy consent, 123
Expert opinion, 222
Experts, neutral, in lawsuit settlement, 189
Expert witnesses
  credentials for, 79
  cross-examination of, 181, 183
  for defendant, 164
  defined, 222
  depositions by, 180
  in medical malpractice cases
    gastric stapling, 33–34
    orthopaedic surgery, 40–41
    proximate cause, 37–39
    and standard of care, 32–36, 55, 56
    vein catheterization, 55, 56
  for plaintiff, 167, 176, 179–183
  "professional," 180–181
  qualifications of, 70, 180
  versus *res ipsa loquitur*, 34–36
  specialties of, 180
  testimony of
    conflicting, 159
    discrediting, 176, 179–183
    training and experience of, 180–181
    treatment as, avoiding, 167

Exploratory surgery malpractice case, 26–27
Express consent, 218
Express contracts, 44–47
Extended reporting endorsements, 100–102, 238
Eyebrow positioning malpractice case, 38–39

Facial implants malpractice case, 61–62
Fact-finding in dispute resolution, 189
False testimony, 232
Family members (of patients)
  diagnostic test results provided to, 148
  in informed consent, 116, 118
  during litigation, 206–208
  in surgeon-patient relationship, 109–110
  after surgery, 114
  surgical briefing of, 113
  written information to, 147
Family relationships and asset protection, 192
Fault-based administrative alternatives to dispute resolution, 75–79
Federal courts, 222
Fellows in training. *See* Residents
Fibrocystic breast disease malpractice case, 43–44
Fiduciaries, 222
Finances, personal (assets), 191–195
Finger deformity malpractice case, 46–47
Firearm discharge reporting, 66
Florida Injured Infants Plan, 86
Follow-up care
  in hysterectomy malpractice case, 27–28
  in medical records, 128, 145
  plans for, documentation of, 131–132
  by residents, 145
  in standard of care, 27–28

Franklin v. Gupta, 53–54
Fraud, 222
Fraudulent misrepresentation, 230
Frequency of claims, 223
Friends of patients, briefing, 113
Frivolous lawsuits, 70, 215
Future earnings, loss of, 40–41, 223

Gallbladder malpractice cases, 26–27, 57–59
Gastric stapling malpractice case, 33–34
General (intangible) damages, 82, 219
Geographic practice limitations, 114
Gifts in asset protection, 193, 194
Gifts to Minors Act, 193
"Going bare" (without insurance), 192–193
Good Samaritan statutes, 63–65, 223
Gross negligence, 79
Guaranty funds, 97, 99, 223
Guardians, 123, 223
Guthrey, Dr., 13
Guzman v. Faraldo, 36–37

Haley v. United States, 29–31
Hand burn malpractice case, 35–36
Harvard University Medical Practice Study of no-fault system costs, 84
Hauser v. Bhatnager, 38–39
Health care providers, 48–54, 139, 147. *See also* Care; Nurses; Residents; Surgeon entries
   accreditation of, 82, 119, 125, 136, 138, 140
Health Care Quality Improvement Act of 1986, 66
Hearing examiners in dispute resolution, 76–77

Heart surgery malpractice cases, 36–37, 181–183
Hemorrhage malpractice cases, 28–29, 55–56
History-taking during office visits, 111–112
Hodgkin's disease treatment, 55–56
Hospital charts. *See* Medical records
Hospitalization, preparing patients for, 112–113
Hospitals. *See also* Health care providers
   chain of command in, 149
   consent forms of, 146
   departments (units) of, 135–141, 149, 220, 240
   house (medical) staffs of, 99–100, 220
   in incident settlement, 187–188
   insurance coverage by, 98, 99
   liability of, 48–54
   policies of, complying with, 147
   quality assurance programs of, 135–141
   residents in, 146–147. *See also* Residents
   risk management by, 135–136, 146–147, 187–188
   risk prevention in, 146–147
   substandard, 82
House calls, 114
House (medical) staff, 99–100, 220, 224
Humane concern expressions, 74
Hypothetical questions, 224
Hysterectomy follow-up malpractice case, 28

Immunity from liability, 63–66, 223, 224
Impaired vision malpractice case, 181–182
Impairment, defined, 224
Implied consent, 218
Implied contracts, 44–45
Important aspects of care, 224

Index

Impressions in medical records, 126–127
Incapacity, 225. *See also* Incompetent *entries*
Incident management, 5–6
Incident reports, 131, 225
Incident settlement, 187–188
Incompetent persons in statutes of limitations, 60–61. *See also* Incapacity; Mentally disabled
Incompetent surgeons, 149–150
Indemnity, 225
Indiana patient compensation fund, 99
Indicators (of important aspects of care), 139–141, 225, 230, 239
Individual retirement accounts (IRAs), 194
Industrial revolution, 12
Infants, compensation for, 86
Infection malpractice case, 29–31
Infectious waste disposal, 130
Information
    communicating, in quality assurance programs, 139–140
    confidential, 66, 217
    not wanted by patients, 116–117
    for patients, 112–113, 117, 144, 146–147
    from patients, gathering, 110–112
    pertinent for informed consent, 115
    withheld from patients, 116–117, 239
Informational aids for patients, 121–123, 128
Informed consent
    in breast surgery malpractice case, 43–44
    defined, 225
    disclosure in, 115, 116, 122–123
    failure to obtain, excuses for, 116–117

family members in, 116, 118
obtaining
    during office visits, 112, 117–118, 122–123, 148
    process of, 115–124, 145–146
    residents in, 145–146
    responsibility for, 118–119
    in special circumstances, 123–124
requirements for, 70
surgeon-patient relationship in, 115–116
Initials in medical records, 126
Injured Infants Act of Virginia, 86
Injured Infants Plan in Florida, 86
Injuries. *See specific entries, eg:* Compensable medical injuries; Vaccine injuries, compensation for
Innocent misrepresentation, 230
Innocent third-party protection from injury, 66
Insolvency planning, 195
Institutional immunity, 224
Insurance
    defined, 225
    liability. *See* Liability insurance; Medical malpractice insurance
    reporting requirement in, 235
    self-, 158, 236
    under-, 192–193
Insurance companies, 98–99, 225
    attorney selection by, 160
    captive, 226
    claim notification of, 158, 202
    commercial, 98, 99
    defined, 226
    insolvent, 97, 99, 223
    in lawsuit settlement, 187–188
    physician–owned, 98
    reserve of, 235
    surcharging (experience rating) by, 104, 222
    surplus line, 99
Insurance coverage, 99–104, 191, 193, 228

Insurance policies
  claims-made, 100–102, 216
    extended reporting endorsements (tail coverage) in, 100–102, 238
  defined, 225, 233
  occurrence, 100–101, 102, 231
Insurance premiums, 15, 97, 99, 104
  claims frequency in, 223
  claims severity in, 237
  defined, 233
  experience ratings for, 104, 222
Insurance rates, 234. See also Insurance premiums
Intangible (general) damages, 82, 219
Integrity of surgeon challenged, 204
Intent, 226
  to sue, notice of, 74
Interpreters for patients, 132
Interrogatories, 162, 220, 226
IRAs (individual retirement accounts), 194

Joint and several liability, 71, 75, 226
Joint College of Physicians and Surgeons of London, 12
Joint Commission on Accreditation of Healthcare Organizations (JCAHO), 82, 119, 125, 136, 138, 140
Joint defense programs for insurance coverage, 99
Jointly titled assets, 193
Joint Underwriting Associations (JUAs), 98, 226
Joyce v. National Medical Registry, Inc., 48–49
Judges. See also Trials
  in dispute settlement, 187–189
  trial, rulings by, 220
Judgments, 227
  assets protected from, 191–192
  based on previous decisions, 237

  in excess of insurance coverage, 191, 193
  summary, 238
Junior attorneys, 160–161
Juravle v. Ozdagler, 57–59
Juries
  in comparative negligence cases, 62–63
  damages awarded by, 40–42, 63, 70–71, 191
  defined, 227
  demeanor affecting, 176–177
  expert testimony evaluated by, 34
  speaking to, 178
  standard of care instructions to, 74
Jury trials, 157, 159, 188–189, 227

Kearns v. Superior Court, 64–65
Kentucky Medical Insurance Company, 84
KEOGH plans, 194
King's Bench, 11
Kirschner's wires malpractice case, 59–60
Knee malignancy court case, 18

Laboratory reports in medical records, 130
Laminectomy malpractice case, 51–52
Law
  defined, 227
  matter of, 229
Lawsuits, 215. See also Covenants not to sue; Litigation; Medical malpractice claims
  complaint in, 157–159, 201–205, 217, 233
  counter-, 74
  defined, 227
  frivolous, 70, 215
  history of, 11
  motions in, 230
  notice of, 74
  plaintiffs in, 232
  pleadings in, 233

Index

Lawsuits *(continued)*
   settlement of. *See* Settlement of lawsuits
   summonses in, 157, 158, 238
   unwarranted, 158
   for wrongful death, 240
Lawyers. *See* Attorneys
Leg amputation malpractice case, 40–41
Legal counsel. *See* Attorneys
Legal disputes. *See specific entries, eg:* Alternative dispute resolution; Lawsuits; Mediation of disputes
Liability
   for acts of others, 47–54, 144n, 193
   contract, 44–47
   for damages, 68, 71–72, 74, 75, 226
   defined, 228
   of employers, 48–50, 144n, 193, 236, 240
   immunity from, 63–66, 223, 224
   joint and several, 71, 75, 226
   malpractice, 30–31, 73. *See also* Medical malpractice *entries*
   personal, 192, 193
   product, 43
   redefining, 79
   of residents, 103, 143–144
   of supervisors of residents, 143–144
   vicarious, 48–54, 144n, 240
Liability insurance, 3, 67. *See also* Medical malpractice insurance
Licenses, 228
Licensing authorities, 66, 186
Life-support systems, 123
Limitations statutes. *See* Statutes of limitations
Limits of coverage in insurance, 228. *See also* Insurance coverage
Litigation. *See also* Lawsuits; Medical malpractice claims
   defined, 157, 228

   medical malpractice crises in, 3, 14–15, 67, 74
   stipulations in, 238
Litigation Assistant (American College of Obstetricians and Gynecologists), 6
Locality (community standard) rule, 21–22, 228
Longman v. Jasiek, 19–20
Loss control, 6, 135
Loss of consortium, 39–40, 82, 229
Lung tumor malpractice case, 41–42

McCord v. Maguire, 26–27
MacGuineas v. United States, 55–56
Malignancies. *See* Cancer malpractice cases
Malpractice, defined, 159, 167, 229. *See also* Medical malpractice *entries*
Mastectomy malpractice case, 13. *See also* Breast surgery malpractice cases
Masters and servants. *See* Agency relationship; Captain of the ship doctrine; *Respondeat superior* doctrine; Vicarious liability doctrine
Matter of law, 229
Matter of record, 229
Mediation of disputes, 187, 189, 229
Medical boards, 75–79, 82
   licensing, 66. *See also* Licensing authorities
Medical certainty, reasonable degree of, 235
Medical emergencies. *See* Emergency *entries*
Medical Malpractice: A Primer for Physicians (Danner), 125, 170
Medical malpractice claims, 20–32. *See also* Claims *entries*; Lawsuits; Litigation; Trials

Medical malpractice claims (continued)
  alternative dispute resolution of, 75–87, 214
  breach of professional standards or abandonment as basis for, 19–20
  damages in. See Damages, in medical malpractice claims
  defense in, development of, 159
  defenses against. See Defenses against malpractice claims
  evaluating, 76, 77
  frivolous, 70, 215
  history of, 13–16
  initiation of, 68, 72
  without insurance, 192–193
  insurance company notification of, 158
  management of. See Claims management
  materials related to, handling, 131
  meaning of, changing, 205
  preparing for, 205
  process of, 202, 203, 205–209
  psychological trauma of. See Psychological trauma of medical malpractice claims
  specific. See specific entries, eg: Cancer malpractice cases; Gastric stapling malpractice case
  standard of care in. See Standard of care, in medical malpractice claims
  surgeon participation in, 157–195
  time frame for, 56–61, 202, 203. See also Statutes of limitations
Medical malpractice insurance, 95, 97–104. See also Insurance entries
  American College of Surgeons activities involving, 3–6
  availability of, 97, 98
  choosing, 97, 104
  coverage in
    forms of, 100–104
    limits on, 99–100, 103
  history of, 11–12
  judgments in excess of, 191, 193
  not carrying, results of, 192–193
  premiums for. See Insurance premiums
  for residents, 101–104
Medical malpractice laws, history of, 11–15
Medical malpractice liability, 30–31, 73. See also Liability
Medical malpractice litigation, crises in, 3, 14–15, 67, 74. See also Lawsuits; Litigation; Medical malpractice claims
Medical malpractice reporting requirements, 186
Medical peer review, 65
Medical Professional Review Board, proposed, 82
Medical records
  answers during trial based on, 179
  changes in, 127
  diagnostic test results in, 130, 148
  documentation in, 125–128, 130, 149
  duplicating and referencing, 162–164, 166
  for expert witnesses, 164
  follow-up care in, 145
  housekeeping of, 130
  as legal evidence, 162
  maintenance of, 133
  prescriptions in, 128, 130
  studying, 162–163, 166, 169, 176
  telephone calls in, 130
Medical review panels, 72
Medical societies, 86, 98, 120
Medical (house) staffs, 99–100, 220, 224
Medical technology, access to, 22
Medications, 128–130
Memory answers, 169, 179

Index

Mental anguish, compensation for, 82
Mentally disabled, 60–61, 123. *See also* Incapacity; Incompetent *entries*
Merrill v. Albany Medical Center Hospital, 41–42
Military malpractice cases, 23–26
Mini-trials in dispute resolution, 189
Minors, defined, 229. *See also* Child(ren)
Misrepresentation, 230
Momsen v. Nebraska Methodist Hospital, 28
Monetary damages. *See* Damages
Monitoring of data, 230
Moonlighting by residents, 103
Mort, J., 11
Motions, 230
 dismissal of, 221

Nasogastric feeding tube malpractice case, 61–62
National Cancer Institute study of catheter systems, 55
National Practitioner Data Bank, 69, 186
National standards of care, 147
National Vaccine Injury Compensation Program, 85–86
Negative events, 6, 126, 135, 139
Negligence. *See also Res ipsa loquitur* doctrine
 comparative, 15, 62–63, 71, 231
 contributory, 62, 63, 231
 defined, 20, 230–231
 of employees, 48–50, 144n, 193, 236, 240
 gross versus ordinary, 79
 in medical malpractice claims, 20–32. *See also* Medical malpractice *entries*
 of patients, 61–63
 and standard of care, 230–231
 as tort, 13

Negligent misrepresentation, 230
Nerve damage malpractice cases, 38–39
Neurologic injuries of infants, 86
Neutral experts in lawsuit settlement, 189
New York, insurance policies in, 101
New Zealand Accident Compensation Corporation, 84–85
Next of kin, 40. *See also* Family members
Niccoli v. Thompson, 31–32
No-fault compensation, 81–87, 99, 103, 217, 232
Norman Conquest, 11
Noto v. St. Vincent's Hospital & Medical Center, 50
Nurses
 care provided by, 139
 in informed consent, 119
 medical record notes by, 128

Occurrence policies, 100–101, 102, 231
O'Connell, Jeffrey, 79–81
Office records. *See* Medical records
Office visits
 informed consent during, 112, 117–118, 122–123, 148
 return, in medical records, 127
 in surgeon-patient relationship, 110–112
Offices
 operations of, reviewing, 132
 patient attitudes toward, 132
 risk management in, 148
 in risk prevention, 129–133
Omnibus consent provision, 121–122
Open heart surgery malpractice case, 36–37
Operations. *See* Surgery; Surgical *entries*
Opinions in medical records, 126–127
Oral surgeon malpractice case, 19–20

"Ordinance Against Malpractice" of Joint College of Physicians and Surgeons of London, 12
Ordinary negligence, 79
Orthopaedic surgeon malpractice case, 40–41
Osteomyelitis malpractice case, 19–20
Out-of-pocket (special) damages, 219
Outpatient settings. *See also* Office visits; Offices
  risk management in, 148
  risk prevention in, 129–133
Ovarian tumor malpractice case, 64–65

Pace method of gastric stapling, 34
Pain
  and informed consent, 123
  and suffering, 41, 82, 231
Pamphlets as informational aid, 121–123
Pancreatic cancer malpractice case, 24–26, 32
Paraplegic malpractice case, 51–52
Paresthesia after eyebrow surgery, 38
Partnerships, 232
Patient charts. *See* Medical records
Patient compensation funds (PCFs), 81–87, 99, 103, 217, 232. *See also* Compensation, for damages
Patients
  abandonment of, 19–20, 114, 213
  attitudes of, evaluating, 132
  choosing, 148
  compliance by, lack of, 127
  confidence of, in surgeons, 109–110. *See also* Surgeon-patient relationship
  continuing care instructions for, 148
  dissatisfaction of, 131
  family members of. *See* Family members (of patients)
  friends of, briefing, 113
  information for, 112–113, 117, 144, 146–147
  information withheld from, 116, 239
  interactions with, during litigation, 206–208
  negligence of, 61–63
  postoperative representative designated by, 113
  preparing for surgery, 112–113
  rapport with, 132–133
  and residents, 144–148
  termination of, 18–20, 131, 213
Patient Safety Manual (American College of Surgeons), 3, 121–122
PCFs (patient compensation funds), 81–87, 99, 103, 217, 232. *See also* Compensation, for damages
Peer review, 65
Pennsylvania patient compensation fund, 99
Pension plans, 194
Performance related to indicators, 140–141
Performance reviews of physicians, 78, 79
Period of repose, 59–61, 232
Periodic payments of damages, 72, 75, 232
Perjury, 232
Personal
  finances (assets), 191–195
  immunity, 224
  liability, 192, 193
  mastery in coping with lawsuits, 204–205
Persuasive speaking, 177–178
Physical examinations during office visits, 112
Physical illness during litigation, 206
Physician-owned insurance companies, 98–99

Index

Physician-patient privilege, 217. *See also* Surgeon-patient relationship
Physician performance reviews, 78, 79
Piercing the corporate veil, 193
Plaintiffs, 232
   attorneys of, 165–166, 168–171
   expert witnesses for, 167, 176, 179–183
Plastic surgeon malpractice cases, 38–39, 181–182
Plato, 11
Pleadings, 233
Policies. *See* Insurance policies
Port-A-Cath system, 55–56
Possibility, defined, 233
Postoperative malpractice cases, 27–32
Postoperative period, 27–32, 113–114
Postoperative rounds, 114
Practice profiles of surgical staff, 140
Practicing Surgeon's Perspective, The (Brittain), 125
Prejudice in damage awards, 41–42
Premiums. *See* Insurance premiums
Preponderance of the evidence, 21
Prescriptions, 128–130
Pretreatment contracts, 79
Pretrial screening, 72, 233
Prima facie
   case, defined, 234
   defined, 234
   evidence, defined, 222
Principals and agents, 47–54, 144n, 213. *See also* Captain of the ship doctrine; *Respondeat superior* doctrine; Vicarious liability doctrine
Prisoners in statutes of limitations, 60–61
Private contracts, 79
Privilege, therapeutic, 239
Probability, defined, 234

Problem correction in quality assurance, 141
Problem situations for residents, 148–149
Procedural defenses against malpractice claims, 56–63
Procedures, surgical. *See* Surgery
Product liability cases, 43
Professional demeanor, 167–168, 175–177
Professional disciplinary action, immunity from, 66
"Professional" expert witnesses, 180–181
Professional liability. *See* Liability; Medical malpractice *entries*
Professional liability insurance. *See* Insurance *entries*; Medical malpractice insurance
Professionals, qualifications of, 234
Professional standards, breach of, 19–20
Professional work, control over, 209, 210
Profiles of surgical staff, 140
Prognosis, patient not wanting, 117
Property transfers, 192–195
Prosthetic device malpractice cases, 40–41, 61–62, 181–182
Providers. *See* Insurance companies
Providing Management Information for Patient Safety Programs (American College of Surgeons), 3
Proximate cause, 36–39, 215
Psychiatrist malpractice case, 50
Psychological trauma of medical malpractice claims, 199, 201–212
   complaint in, 201–205
   coping with, 202–205, 207–211
   expectations about, 202, 206–207, 209–210
   litigation process in, 205–209

255

Psychological trauma *(continued)*
  litigation resolution in, 209–212
Publication of defamatory material, 234
Pulmonary edema malpractice case, 28–29
Punitive/exemplary damages, 39–40, 42–44, 72–73, 82, 219
Purchasing (risk retention) groups, 99, 236
Pure risk, 236

Qualifications
  of expert witnesses, 70, 180
  of professionals, 234
Quality assurance
  committees, 136
  coordinators, 138
  defined, 234
  programs, 132, 135–141
Questions
  answering, 167–171, 178–179
  during depositions, 167–171
  hypothetical, 224
  in interrogatories, 226
  misleading or tricky, 170–171, 179
  during trials, 158–159, 178–179

Rates (insurance), 234. *See also* Insurance premiums
Reager v. Anderson, 40–41
Reasonable, defined, 234
Reasonable degree of medical certainty, defined, 235
Receptionists in surgeon-patient relationship, 110
Recordkeeping. *See* Documentation; Medical records
Rectal stump malpractice case, 29–31
Referrals, 29–31
  versus consultations, 218
  in medical records, 127
Releases, 185, 235
Repetition in testimony, 178

Reporting endorsements (tail coverage), 100–102, 238
Reporting requirement in insurance, 235
Repose
  period of, 59–61, 232
  statute of. *See* period of, *above*
Reputation attacked in trials, 173–174
Reserve of insurance companies, 235
Residents
  accountability of, 143–144
  care by, 145, 149. *See also* standard of care for, *below*
  emergency overruling of impaired surgeons by, 150
  ethical issues addressed by, 148–150
  in hospital setting, 146–147
  in informed consent process, 145–146
  insurance coverage for, 101–104
  liability of, 103, 143–144
  moonlighting by, 103
  in outpatient/office setting, 148
  and patients, 144–148
  practice limitations for, 103
  problem situations for, 148–149
  requests of, not to perform surgery, 149
  in risk prevention, 143–150
  standard of care for, 144, 147
  status of, 144
  supervision of, 143–145
Res ipsa loquitur doctrine, 34–36, 73, 235–236
Respondeat superior doctrine, 48–50, 144n, 236
Retirement assets, 194
Return visits in medical records, 127
Rights
  defined, 236
  of surgeons, 114
Risk financing, 5, 95, 97–104. *See also* Insurance *entries*

Index

Risk management
  defined, 5, 236
  by hospitals, 135–136, 146–147, 187–188
  in outpatient/office setting, 148
Risk management committees, 136
Risk pooling by Joint Underwriting Associations, 98, 226
Risk prevention, 4–5, 107, 109–150
  consent in, 115–124
  defined, 135
  departments of surgery in, 135–141
  medical record documentation in, 125–128
  versus quality assurance, 135–136
  quality assurance programs in, 135–141
  residents in, 143–150
  surgeon-patient relationship in, 109–114
Risk retention groups, 99, 236
Risks
  in consent forms, 119–121
  defined, 236
  evaluating and classifying (underwriting), 98, 226, 240
  of judgments in excess of insurance coverage, 191, 193
  patients informed about, 117, 146–147
  patients not wanting information about, 116–117
  pure, 236
  recordkeeping of, 118
  speculative, 236
  of underinsurance, 192–193
Roman law, 11
Rounds, postoperative, 114
Rural practitioners, 21–22

St. Paul Insurance Company, 98
Scarzella v. Saxon, 45–46
Schaffner v. Cumberland County Hospital, 35–36

Screening, pretrial, 72, 233
Sealed settlement offers, 76
Secretary's Commission of U.S. Department of Health and Human Services, 14
Sedation and informed consent, 123
Self-assessment exercises, 132
Self-esteem in coping with lawsuits, 204–205
Self-insurance, 158, 236
Servants. *See* Agency relationship; Borrowed servant doctrine
Settlement of lawsuits, 75–87, 185–189, 214
  defined, 185, 237
  incident, 187–188
  structured, 237
Severity of claims (claim magnitude), 237
Sexual relationship malpractice case, 50
Sexually transmitted disease reporting, 66
Shock and informed consent, 123
"Shotgun tactics," 71
Shoulder wires malpractice case, 59–60
Signatures
  on consent forms, 121
  on medical records, 126
Silicone implants malpractice case, 61–62
Social support in coping with lawsuits, 203–204, 208, 209
Somatic reactions after litigation resolution, 210
Southwick, Arthur, 53
Special (out-of-pocket) damages, 219
Specialists
  practice restriction by, 114
  and standard of care, 22
  sub-, referral to. *See* Referrals
  in training, standards of care for, 147. *See also* Residents

Specialties of expert witnesses, 180
Specific memory answers, 169, 179
Speculation during trial, 179
Speculative risk, 236
Spouses
  damages awarded to, 40
  gifts of assets to, 194
  loss of consortium by, 229
  personal liabilities of, 192
  for social support, 208, 209
  surviving, 40
  tenancy by the entirety between, 193
Squamous cell carcinoma malpractice case, 31–32
Staff training, 130
Standard of care
  care and treatment in, 26–27
  defined, 21, 167, 237
  diagnosis in, 22–26
  locality rule in, 228
  in medical malpractice claims, 21–31
    adherence to, as defense, 54–56
    expert testimony about, 32–36
    instructions to juries about, 74
    and tort reform, 68, 70, 72, 73
    and unnecessary surgery, 31–32
  national, 147
  and negligence, 230–231
  in pretreatment contracts, 79
  and proximate cause, 36–39
  referrals in, 29–31
  for residents, 144, 147
  significant deviation from, 32–36, 159, 167, 229
  in vein catheterization death, 55–56
Stare decisis doctrine, 12, 237
State medical associations. *See* Medical boards; Medical societies
Statistics in consent forms, 121

Statutes of limitations, 56–61
  defined, 237
  discovery rule in, 57–61, 220
  limitations on, 71, 75
  period of repose in, 59–61, 232
Statutory immunities against liability, 63–66, 223
Sterilization consent, 123
Stipulations in litigation, 238
Structured settlement of lawsuits, 237
Study commissions for medical malpractice liability, 73
Subpoenas, 131, 238
Subspecialists, referral to. *See* Referrals
Substantive defenses against malpractice claims, 54–56
Substantive tort law. *See* Medical malpractice laws, history of; Tort *entries*
Suits. *See* Lawsuits; Litigation; Medical malpractice claims
Summary judgment, 238
Summary jury trials, 188–189
Summonses in lawsuits, 157, 158, 238
Supervisors of residents, 143–145
Supraorbital nerve damage malpractice case, 38–39
Surcharging by insurance companies, 104, 222
Surgeon-attorney relationship, 157–164, 176
Surgeon-patient relationship, 17–20
  confidentiality in, 66, 217
  express contracts in, 45
  in informed consent, 115–116
  office visits in, 110–112
  patient preparation for surgery in, 112–113
  postoperative period in, 113–114
  in risk prevention, 5–6, 109–114
  terminating, 18–20, 131, 213

Index

Surgeons. *See specific entries, eg:* Defendants, surgeons as; Rights, of surgeons

Surgery
 departmental protocols for, 149
 departments of, 135–141, 149
 and postoperative period, 27–32, 113–114
 preparing patients for, 112–113
 resident request not to perform, 149
 results of, in consent form, 121
 risks of
  in consent form, 119–121
  recordkeeping of, 118
 types of. *See specific entries, eg:* Eyebrow positioning malpractice case; Heart surgery malpractice case
 unnecessary, 31–32
Surgical competence in risk prevention, 5
Surgical professional liability insurance. *See* Liability insurance; Medical malpractice insurance
Surgical staff, profiles of, 140
Surplus line insurance companies, 99
Surviving spouses, 40
Sweden
 no-fault medical injury system in, 84, 85
 preferred therapy identification in, 83
Symbols in medical records, 126
Sympathy in damage awards, 41–42

Tail coverage (extended reporting endorsements), 100–102, 238
Telephone calls, 127–130
Tenancy by the entirety, 193
Testimony. *See also* Expert opinion; Expert witnesses; Witnesses
 communication clarity in, 178–179
 conflicting, 159
 of defendants, 177–179
 defined, 239
 discrediting, 176, 179–183
 false, 232
 inconsistencies in, 174–176
 repetition in, 178
Textbook references, authoritative, 171, 179
Therapeutic privilege, 116, 239
Thresholds for evaluation, 140–141, 239
Tonelli v. Khanna, 43–44
Tooth extraction malpractice case, 19–20
Tort law, 5–87
 changes in, 14, 15, 75–87
 versus criminal law, 12
 development of, 12–13
 history of, 11–15
 medical-legal concepts in, 17–66. *See also specific entries, eg:* Medical malpractice claims; Negligence; Surgeon-patient relationship
Tort reform, 14, 15, 67–75, 215, 233
 defined, 239
Torts, defined, 20, 239
Transfers to Minors Act, 193
Transplant consent, 123
Treatment
 alternate, 54
 for complications, in medical records, 128
 consent to. *See* Consent; Consent forms; Informed consent
 continuing, in statutes of limitations, 71
 contracts covering, 79
 discussion of
  with family members, 118
  with patients, 117
 experimental, 123
 methods of, refusing, 114
 optimal, determining, 83
 plans for, in medical records, 126–127

Treatment (continued)
  recommendations for, during office visits, 112
  risks and complications of, patients informed about, 146–147
  in standard of care, 26–27, 54
Trial courts, 214, 239
Trial judges, 220
Trials, 173–183. See also Lawsuits; Litigation
  court (bench), 219
  defendant in
    demeanor of, 175–177
    emotional reactions of, 174, 176–177
    presence of, 174–176
    reputation attacked, 173–174
  defined, 239
  deposition statements in, 166
  jury, 157, 159, 188–189, 227
  planning and preparing for, 174–176
  questions during, 158–159, 178–179
  speculation during, 179
  testimony in. See Expert witnesses; Testimony; Witnesses
  textbook references during, 179
Trusts in asset protection, 194

Ulcerative colitis malpractice case, 29–31
Umbrella insurance coverage, 191
Unavailability, right of, 114
Underinsurance, 192–193
Underwriting, 98, 226, 240
Unforeseen conditions in consent form, 121
Units (departments) of hospitals, 135–141, 149, 220, 240
Unwarranted lawsuits, 158
Urethra diverticulum malpractice case, 45–46
Urinary problem malpractice case, 31–32

U.S. Department of Health and Human Services, Secretary's Commission of, 14

Vaccine injuries, compensation for, 85–86
Valentine v. Thomas, 59–60
Valve replacement malpractice case, 181–182
Van Zee v. Witzke, 46–47
Vein catheterization malpractice case, 55–56
Verdicts, 70–71, 240
  directed, 220
Vertebral artery malpractice case, 181–182
Veterans Administration Hospital in malpractice case, 25–26, 32
Vicarious liability doctrine, 48–54, 144n, 240
Videotapes as informational aid, 121–123
Virginia compensation system for injured infants, 86
Vision impairment malpractice case, 181–182
Vulvectomy malpractice case, 31–32

Warranty, breach of, 46
Waste disposal, 130
Weekly v. Solomon, 33–34
Wheat v. United States, 23–24
Whipple procedure, 26
Wires in shoulder malpractice case, 59–60
Witnesses
  defined, 240
  expert. See Expert witnesses
  subpoenas for, 238
Written consent, 240
Wrongful death, 240

X-ray reports, 130, 132